Wilson Harvey/Loewy

Part of the Loewy Group

>

>

ROCKPORT

1000

1000 Type Treatments.

From script to serif, letterforms used to perfection.

>
>

>
>
>

First published in the
United States of America by
Rockport Publishers, Inc.
a member of
Quayside Publishing Group
33 Commercial Street
Gloucester
Massachusetts   01930-5089

Telephone   (978) 282-9590
Fax   (978) 283-2742

www.rockpub.com

ISBN 1-59253-159-8

10 9 8 7 6 5 4 3 2 1

Design   WilsonHarvey/Loewy
                +44 (0)20 7798 2098

Printed in China
Printed in Singapore

Design, research, judging
Paul Burgess.
Ben Wood.

Artwork
Peter Usher.

Additional photography
Kev Dutton at Fotofit.

Fonts
Helvetica Neue.

Introduction.

1000 Type Treatments

DIE ERDE STIRBT NICHT VON SELBST. SIE
WIRD GETÖTET. UND DIE TÄTER HABEN
NAMEN UND ADRESSEN.

UTAH PHILLIPS

Designers who push the boundaries of type are not a new phenomena. El Lissitzky, Moholy-Nagy, Futurism, Dadaism, de Stijl, and members of the Bauhaus all helped to kick-start typographic experimentation and develop the foundation of typographic refinement. Every decade has given us a new approach, as well as a new appreciation of how to handle type. Not unlike what is done in the music industry, it is easy for us to be retrospective, labeling eras by their associated trends. It is much harder, however, to be introspective, and determine what defines typography today. To find out, we need to stand back and take a snapshot of how designers and typographers across the world are tackling type. Each designer has his or her personal influences and inspirations; each pushes his or her work, clients, and peers; and each designer influences the ways in which type is treated today, and how it will be treated in the future.

Art and popular culture have led us through an era of postmodernism and, more recently, "shockism." This movement has subsequently influenced design, resulting in typographic experimentation and an age of calligraphic freedom— a backlash to the digital design age. Typographers are once more enjoying a freedom to explore that technology has spent so long hindering. That said, clarity, structure, and information handling still, and will always, have their place in today's eclectic design mix, proving there is still plenty of room for subtlety, beauty, and refinement.

Typography is a niche, it is a passion, and it's often a field for huge debate and banter amongst those who care about it. But type is essential: it directs us, it clarifies information, and it coerces us to buy products— impressive accolades for an area of design so often overlooked by the public.

Unsurprisingly, the layman would find the idea of 1,000 different type treatments an incomprehensible, peculiar notion that, at the end of the day, is of little or no interest. To those of us in the design community with an eye for typographic excellence, the idea of a tome dedicated entirely to capturing the world's most exquisite typographic detail is nothing short of tantalizing.

Nondesigners have little idea how much typography affects their daily lives—which is not really a bad thing, as it means we're doing our jobs well. But to the designers who spend their lives making type work for the rest to ignore, this book is for you— I hope it inspires. For everyone else, I hope it sparks an appreciation, an understanding, and above all, a passion for type.

Paul Burgess
WilsonHarvey/Loewy

>

>

Chapter 1.
Flyers + leaflets.

1800

Postcards
>

Flyers

Mailers

Leaflets
>

Handouts

0002
ALR Design
USA
↘

0003
Miriello Grafico, Inc.
USA
↘↘

0004
Joe Miller's Company
USA
↘

0005
Graphiculture
USA
↘↘

0006
ALR Design
USA
↘

0007
ALR Design
USA
↘↘

008/009
1000
Flyers +
leaflets

0002

0004

0006

0003

0005

0007

0008
CDT Design Ltd
UK

0009
Ideation Signs & Communications, Inc.
USA

0010
Ideation Signs & Communications, Inc.
USA

0011
Ideation Signs & Communications, Inc.
USA

0012
LSD
Spain

0013
LSD
Spain

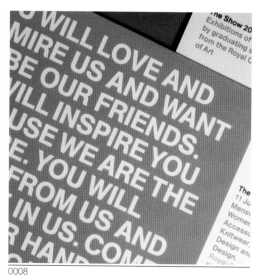

0008

0010

0012

0009

0011

0013

0014
_SD
Spain

0015
LSD
Spain

0016
LSD
Spain

0017
LSD
Spain

010/011
1000
Flyers +
leaflets

TORTURA COMO ARMA DE GUERRA:
LA MAYORIA DE LAS VICTIMAS
DE LAS GUERRAS ACTUALES
SON CIVILES, NO SOLDADOS.
EN LOS CONFLICTOS MODERNOS,
EL ATERRORIZAR A LA POBLACION
CIVIL SE HA CONVERTIDO EN
UN MEDIO HABITUAL DE GUERRA,
UN MEDIO QUE, CASI
INVARIABLEMENTE, IMPLICA
EL USO DE LA TORTURA. www.a-i.es

0014

0016

abcdef
ghijkl
mnñop
qrstu
vwxyz

ABCDEF
GHIJKL
MNÑOP
QRSTU
VWXYZ

Geoffrey Lee designed impacto in 1965.
Use impacto in display situations requiring a strong statement. / www.lsdspace.com

¡IMPACTO

0015

0017

0018
Christine Fent, Manja Uellpap, Gilmar Wendt
UK

0019
Miriello Grafico, Inc.
USA

0020
Christine Fent, Manja Uellpap, Gilmar Wendt
UK

0021
Miriello Grafico, Inc.
USA

0018

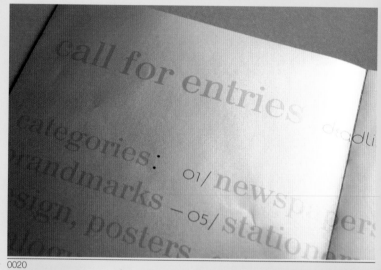

0020

0019

0021

0023
LSD
Spain
↙

0024
LSD
Spain
↘↘

0025
LSD
Spain
↙

0026
LSD
Spain
↘↘

0027
LSD
Spain
↙

0028
LSD
Spain
↘↘

xix fu

xo ex xólo pobrexa ecoxómica (mex
"xer pobre ex texer hambre, carece
ropx, extar exfermo y xo xer atexdi
y xo recibir formxción; xupoxe vulx
hax adverxidadex y a mexudo padec
y excluxióx de hax ixxtitucioxex".
xxxx futurx (dexpuéx de paul rexxe
0023

xel
derechox humaxxox = xxxx futurx   www.tx
0025

ᴓbcdefghi
ᴓñopqrxt
xyz.xxxx fu
lxdxplxce.com
FUTURX xxxx
PQRXTUVW
DEFGHIJKLM
0027

fraterxidax
libertad
iguxldxd
ixhumaxid

derechox humxxxox = xxxx futurx   ww
0024

ixmigraxtex-ixdoc
xxxx futurx: ley de extraxjeríx, 8/2000.

Exta ley ha recortado lox derechox de lox i
-elimixaxdo lox derechox de reuxióx, max
xixdicaxcióx y huelga- y ha reimplaxtado la e
xix permixo de rexidexciax. Focaliza la atex
ha dixcrecioxalidad admixixxtrativa. La vía x
de trabajo coxtixúa xiexdo el xixtema de
ha chtxuxba de prioridad xacioxal, lox pue
de mexor remuxeraxcióx, coxdicioxex labo
0026

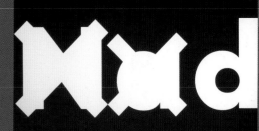
Xxd
derechox humxxxox = xxxx futurx   ww
0028

0029 LSD Spain

0030 LSD Spain

0031 LSD Spain

0032 LSD Spain

0033 Yanek Iontef Israel

0034 Yanek Iontef Israel

014/015 1000 Flyers + leaflets

0029

abc
RSTUVW

0030

las palabras y las imágenes
que utilizamos deben

signi

aquello que decimos y pensamos.

0031

otis sans perfek

la rotis sans serif diseñada por otl aicher

bcdefghijklmnñ
STUVWXYZ

www.lsdspace.com

0032

rotis sans pe

nativa de la rotis sans serif diseñada por otl aicher

rot
S perfekt

www.lsdspace

0033

0034

0035
D-Fuse
UK
↘

0036
Form Fünf Bremen
Germany
↘↘

0037
WilsonHarvey/Loewy
UK
↘

0038
Strichpunkt
Germany
↘↘

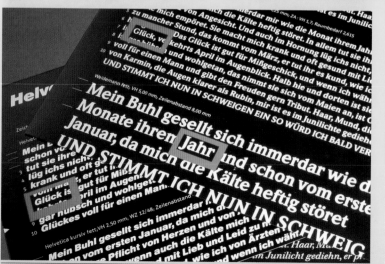

0035

0037

0036

0038

0039
Struktur Design
UK

0040
Strichpunkt
Germany

0041
Untitled
UK

016/017
1000
Flyers +
leaflets

0046
Unreal
UK

0047
Unreal
UK

0048
Q
Germany

0049
Unreal
UK

020/021
1000
Flyers +
leaflets

0050
Blok Design
Mexico
↘

0051
David Salafia/Laura Salafia
USA
↘↘

0052
Blok Design
Mexico
↘

0053
6ixthFloor Projects
USA
↘↘

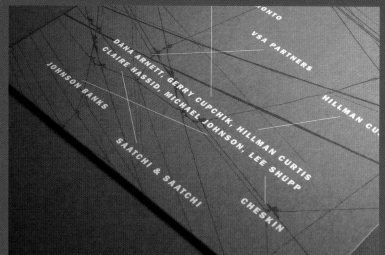

0050

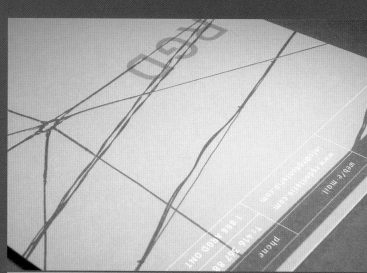

0052

0051

0053

0054
Miriello Grafico, Inc.
USA
↘

0055
Miriello Grafico, Inc.
USA
↘↘

0056
Miriello Grafico, Inc.
USA
↘

0057
Miriello Grafico, Inc.
USA
↘↘

022/023
1000
Flyers +
leaflets

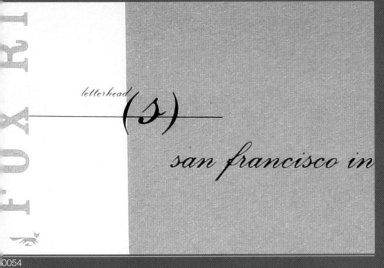

0054

0056

0055

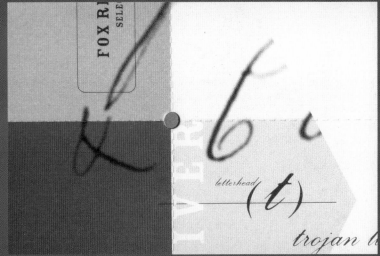

0057

0058

0059

0060

LO SIMPLE
ES
OCULTAR
LA VERDAD

Linus (després de Adrian Frutiger)

0061

A DIDAS, BAY
SIEMENS, SH
MCDONALD'S
SAMSUNG...

¿CUÁNTAS DE NUESTRAS MARCA
SUS GANANCIAS EN LA CORRUP
LA DESTRUCCIÓN DEL MEDIO AM
EL MALTRATO DE ANIMALES?

0063

QUÉ SE ESCONDE
DE LAS IMÁGENE
EXITOSAS DE LAS
GRANDES MARCA

CADA VEZ SON MÁS LAS GRANDES EMPR
TRASLADAN SUS FÁBRICAS ALLÍ DONDE PU
CONDICIONES INHUMANAS DE TRABAJO, Q
SE VERGONZADAMENTE DE CRISIS ECONÓ
FLICTOS ARMADOS, QUE TOLERAN LA
TUD Y QUE TRANSGREDEN LA LEY
ES PROBADAMENTE DAÑINO

0065

PODEMOS AYUDAR A LAS EMPRESAS A CA
Y A EXIGIR UNOS NIVELES MÍNIMOS

NIVE
RPORAT

0062

LAS MARCAS
ULTINACIONALES
DOMINAN TODO
SON EL PODER

0064

A BCDEFGHIJ
NÑOPQ RS TU
YZ bcdefgl
ñopq rs tun
oporationv

Lion (després de Adrian Frutiger)

0066

0068
WilsonHarvey/Loewy
UK

0069
Bright Pink
UK

0070
Strichpunkt
Germany

0071
Dulude
Canada

0072
Jan Family
Denmark

0073
Dynamo
Ireland

026/027
1000
Flyers +
leaflets

0068

0070

0072

0069

0071

0073

0074

0076

0075

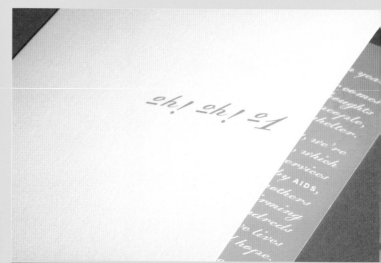

0077

0079

0081

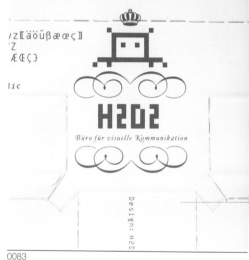

0083

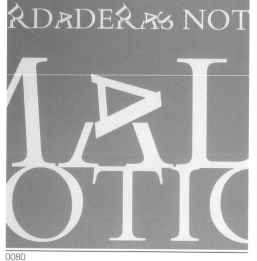

0080

0082

01 02 03 04 05 06 07 08 09 10 11 12
21 22 23 24 25 26 27 28 29 30 31 32
41 42 43 44 45 46 47 48 49 50 51 52

sixty secon

architectu

san francisco

washington unive

0084

0085
Aufuldish & Warinner
USA

0086
**Visuelle
Kommunikation**
Germany

0087
Miriello Grafico, Inc.
USA

0088
Cahan & Associates
USA

030/031
1000
Flyers +
leaflets

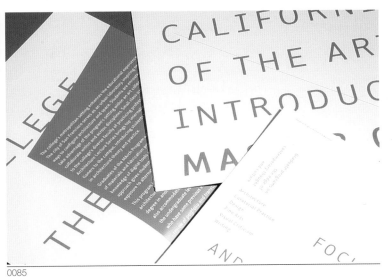

0085

0087

0086

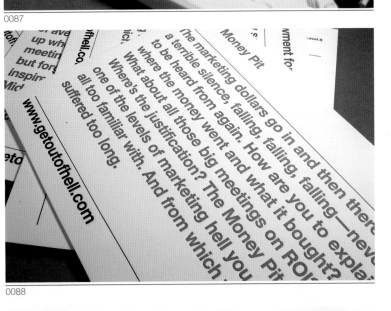

0088

0090
D-Fuse
UK

0091
WilsonHarvey/Loewy
UK

0092
Miriello Grafico, Inc.
USA

0093
A3 Design
USA

032/033
1000
Flyers +
leaflets

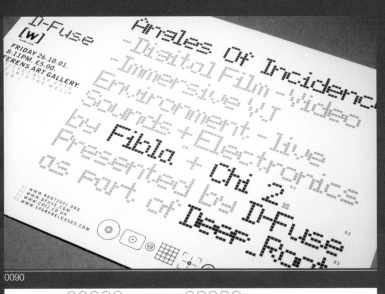

0090

0092

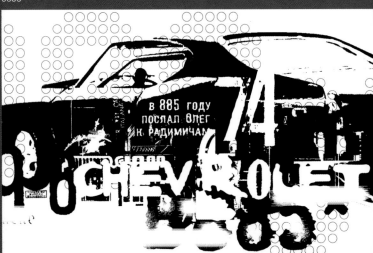

0091

0093

0094

0096

0095

0097

098
Heckman
SA

0099
Untitled
UK

0100
Heckman
USA

0101
Aufuldish & Warinner
USA

034/035
1000
Flyers +
leaflets

0102   0103
Circle K Studio   **Kontour Design**
USA   USA

0104
Jones Design Group
USA

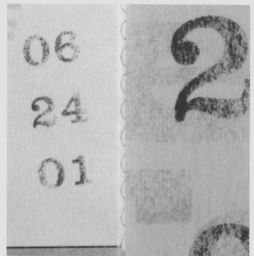

0102

0103

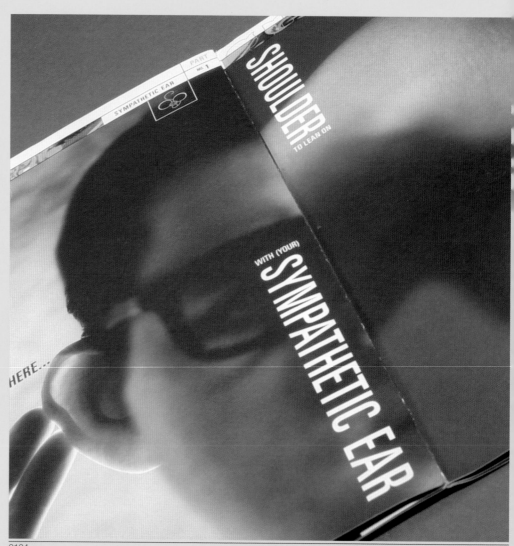

0104

0105   0106
SD   **LSD**
pain   Spain

0107   0108
LSD   **LSD**
Spain   Spain

0109   0110
LSD   **LSD**
Spain   Spain

036/037
1000
Flyers +
leaflets

Utop

0105

Nem todos ter
mas todos mor

Os clochards, sob as pontes de Par's; os nore
os c'ganos, nas caravanas e, embora seja
Auschw'tz. Porque o homem é b'cho que
Há var'as mane'ras de formular tal 'mpos
'nformát'ca e a menos sent'mental'zante.
devemos d'spor de redundânc'as, porque
capta não passa de ruído. E não é possiv'
no caos. A morada e a redundânc'a que n
como também cr'á las a part'r dos ruído
é loucura que leva ao an'qu'lamento.

0107

... are really only two escape'routes from w
'mage or forward to the codes. Back to the 'ma
'nto calculat'on. These reflect'ons put forwa
d'rect'ons can merge surpr's'ngly 'nto one a
be computed to 'mages. From textual wr't'ng,
to escape 'nto 'mag'ned calculat'ons. 'f w
calculat'ng and 'mag'nat've th'nk'ng would be s
th'nk'ng. Wr'ters then would have swallo
mathemat'c'ans and 'mage-makers and thus

onto a new level of

Aven'r Utop'a / www.lsdspace.com   V'lém Flusser. "A

0109

ABCDEFGH'J
PQRSTUVWXY
gh'jklmnñopq

0106

'mag'na

0108

O PATR'OT
S'NT'OM'
ENFERM'
ESTÉT'CA,
TRANSFOR
HÁB'TO EN
M'STER'OSO.

0110

0111　the commissary　USA　↘

0112　the commissary　USA　↘↘

0113　the commissary　USA　↘

0114　the commissary　USA　↘↘

0115　the commissary　USA　↘

0116　the commissary　USA　↘↘

0111

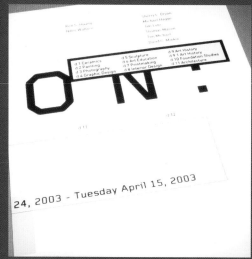

0112

0113

0114

0115

0116

0117

abcdefg
stuwxyz
LMNÑOPQ **RS** TUVWXYZ

www.lsdspace.com

0119

abcd
efghijklm
qrstuwxyz

ABCDEFGHIJKL
MNÑOPQ
STUVWXYZ

Times Sweet Times / www.lsdspace.com

0121

LA TORTURA Y LOS
TRATOS QUE SUFR
MUJERES ESTÁ ENR
EN UNA CUL
UNIVERSAL QUE
A ESTÁS LA IGUALI
DERECHOS CON
HOMBRES Y LEGIT
APROPIA O
VIOLENTA
SU CUER

Times Sweet Times / www.lsdspace.com

0118

OLENCIA CONTRA LA MUJER SE DEF
DE VIOLENCIA BASADO EN LA PERTE
NINO QUE TENGA O PUEDA TENER C
AÑO O SUFRIMIENTO FÍS
OGICO PARA LA MUJER, ASÍ COMO LA
CURRA» Y LA «VIOLENCIA [...] QUE
ES ACTOS, LA COACC

RIVACIÓN ARB
TAD, TANTO SI SE PRODUCEN EN L
EN LA VIDA PRIVADA». INCLUYE LA
TRADA O TOLERADA POR EL ESTAD
CURRA» Y LA «VIOLENCIA [...] QUE
AMILIA» Y EN «LA COMUNIDAD

ARACIÓN SOBRE LA ELIMINACIÓN D

RA LA MUJER.

imes Sweet Times / www.lsdspace.com

0120

VIOLENCIA
TORTU
TERR

EN EL 2000 FUERON
MAS DE 22.000
LAS DENUNCIAS CONTABILIZADAS
EN ESPAÑA POR MALOS TRATOS
A MUJERES

Times Sweet Times / www.lsdspace.com

0122

ltratdos

IA DOMÉSTICA, incluida la violencia
gal, suele considerarse todavía
vado dentro de la familia,
ón de derechos civiles y políticos.
DAD INTERNACIONAL ha reconocido
e la violencia contra las mujeres como
derechos humanos en el que los Estados
sabilidad.

es / www.lsdspace.com

0123
Plus Gestaltung
Germany
↘

0124
Ligalux GmbH
Germany
↘

0126
WilsonHarvey/Loewy
UK

0127
Point Blank
UK

0128
Unreal
UK

0129
WilsonHarvey/Loewy
UK

0126

0128

0127

0129

0130
Sweden Graphics
Sweden

0131
WilsonHarvey/Loewy
UK

0132
WilsonHarvey/Loewy
UK

042/043
1000
Flyers +
leaflets

0130

↘

Electric Weekend.

Electric Avenue Studios & Ritzy Cinema, Brixton
Saturday 26 June / Sunday 27 June 2004

Electric Weekend celebrates the launch
of b3 media's Electric Avenue Studios
in Brixton with a weekend of free
events at the new venue, plus a film
programme at the nearby Ritzy Cinema.
Supported by the Arts Council England,
b3 media is a non-profit multimedia
arts network fostering innovation and
diversity across the arts.

Over two days, groups and individuals
with shared interventionist
sensibilities will take part in
conversations, workshops,
interventions, tactical media
initiatives, social hacking,
noise videos and participatory
artworks. These encounters are geared
towards mapping, connecting and
supporting the diverse media arts
initiatives across London and outside,
focusing on DIY approaches to the
use of public space and technology.

Electric Weekend is a b3 media
production, guest curated by
Lina Dzuverovic-Russell from Electra.
www.electra-productions.com

0134
WilsonHarvey/Loewy
UK

0135
WilsonHarvey/Loewy
UK

0136
WilsonHarvey/Loewy
UK

0137
WilsonHarvey/Loewy
UK

044/045
**1000
Flyers +
leaflets**

0134

0136

0135

0137

0138

0139

0140

0141
Paul Shaw/Letter Design
USA

0142
vo6
Brazil

0143
Aufuldish & Warinner
USA

0144
Rome & Gold Creative
USA

0145
Insight Design
Communications
USA

0146
Kontrapunkt
Denmark

046/047
1000
Flyers +
leaflets

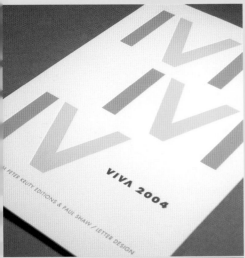

0141

0143

0145

0142

0144

0146

0147
And Partners
USA

0148
344 Design, LLC
USA

0149
344 Design, LLC
USA

0150
Carter Wong Tomlin
UK

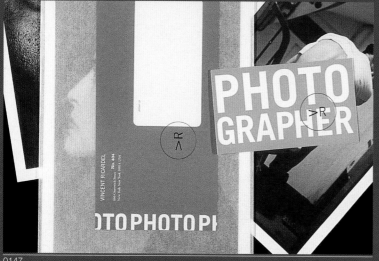

0147

0148

0149

0150

0151
44 Design, LLC
SA

0152
And Partners
USA

0153
And Partners
USA

0154
344 Design, LLC
USA

048/049
1000
Flyers +
leaflets

0151

0153

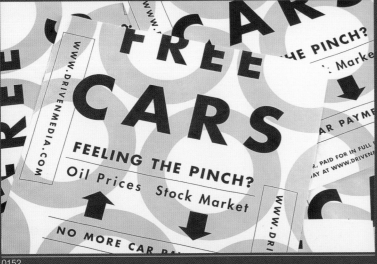

0152

0154

aˮ ¡`ˮ´ç,,-|@#¢¬¬— ˮˮˮˮ´

æ¤®ˮ¥ ø[]åƒ™¶§~

{}®ßµ,,—¡˝˙•£‰ˮŒ/!

Æ‡‡?Ø^ˮ fifl «»

‹›ˮ˚— ŒÆ ¡º‰¿ Å

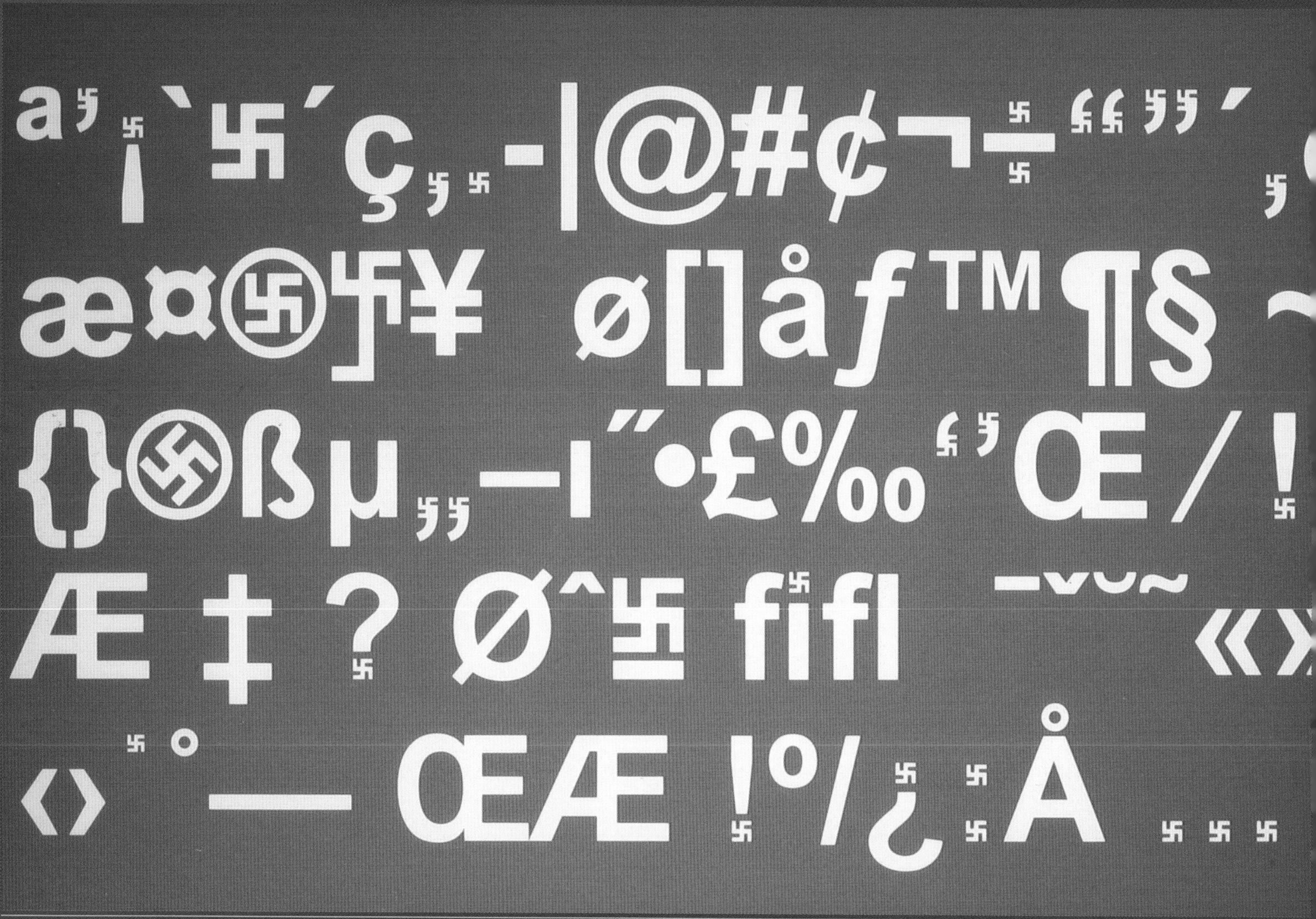

0156   0157
Sweden Graphics   LSD
Sweden   Spain
↓↓   ↓↓

0158   0159
LSD   Sweden Graphics
Spain   Sweden
↓   ↓↓

0160   0161
Sweden Graphics   LSD
Sweden   Spain
↓   ↓↓

050/051 | 1000 Flyers + leaflets

ANTE

INNAN JAG BERÄTTAR DET JAG SKA VILL JAG GE ER EN BAKGRUND: På GYMNASIET VAR JAG MED I EN KLUBB SOM BARA KILLAR FICK VA MED I. VI HADE FRACK OCH LÄSTE DIKTER FÖR VARANN OCH DRACK PUNCH OCH SNUSA LUKTSNUS. KLUBBEN HADE FUNNITS 130 ÅR OCH FOSTRAT MÅNGA DIREKTÖRER, JURISTER OCH AMBASSADÖRER.
TRADITION FÖRPLIKTAR, HERR VON ECKER!
VARSÅGOD, HERR OLSSON ELOQUENTIA!
LÅT OSS SJUNGA PUNCHENS LOV, HERR FAHLÉN FÖR BÖVELEN, HURRA!

Så EN KVÄLL NÄR KLUBBEN HADE MÖTE OCH DEBATTÄMNET VAR KVINNOR HÖRDES SKRIK

UTANFÖR KLUBBLOKALEN[S ...]
OM PINGVINER. VI TITTA[...]
ALLIHOP. DÄR STOD EN SO[...]
VISSTE ATT DEN KILLEN HE[...]
SPELA HOCKEY. HAN VERK[...]
DET GICK GANSKA LÄTT F[...]
DÖRR MED FYRA SPARKA[...]
INGEN AV OSS KUNDE S[...]
HAN FICK IN TVÅ SMÄLL[...]
ANTE SKREK: JAG SKA H[...]
HACKAR MORÖTTER PÅ M[...]
(JUST DET CITATET BLEV [...]
SKÄMT INTERNT I KLUBBE[...]

DET BLEV EN RÄTTEGÅNG,[...]

FAMILJEFRÅGAN

DU ÄTER MIDDAG MED DIN FAMILJ FÖR ATT FIRA ATT DINA FÖRÄLDRAR VARIT GIFTA I 20 ÅR OCH DIN TRET-TONÅRIGA BROR SPILLER UT SITT GLAS MED LÄSK OCH DIN PAPPA HÄRMAR HONOM OCH SPILLER UT SITT GLAS MED VIN ÖVER HELA BORDET OCH DIN BROR BÖRJAR GRÅTA OCH DIN MAMMA SÄGER ATT DET HÄR VAR VÄL EN GANSKA BRA

SAMMANFATTNING AV DOM HÄR 20 ÅREN.

DU ÅKER BIL MED DIN FAMILJ TILL DIN MORMORS 75-ÅRSKALAS OCH DIN 16-ÅRIGA SYSTER VILL STANNA HEM-MA FÖR HENNES KOMPISAR SKA HA FEST OCH HON GRÅTER I BAKSÄTET OCH SÄGER HULKANDE ATT HON INTE VILL FÖLJA MED OCH DIN PAPPA

0156

Hijop
0158

KÄNSLORNA

KÄNSLAN AV ATT SITTA I EN FÖRORTSLÄGENHET MED KABEL MEDAN VÅREN RASAR UTANFÖR KÄNSLAN AV ATT PUGH VAR BÄST PÅ FÖRSTA PLATTAN KÄNSLAN AV ATT VILJA BLI NÅT STORT INNAN MAN DÖR KÄNSLAN AV ATT AKTIEHANDEL ÄR NÅGONTING FEL KÄNSLAN AV ATT LÖRDAGS-HANDLA OCH FÅ SPEL KÄNSLAN AV ATT EGOTRIPPEN

LÅNGT OM LÄNGE GÅR UR KROPPEN OCH DÅ PLÖTSLIGT KÄNNER JAG EN LÄNGTAN EFTER ATT FÅ VA EN LITEN DEL AV NÅGOT BRA

REFR:
//OM DU KÄNNER SOM JAG KÄNNER KÄNNER JAG FÖR DIG OM DU KÄNNER SOM JAG KÄNNER KÄNNER DU FÖR MIG OM DU KÄNNER SOM JAG

ANG. HAT

ÄR PÅ EMMABODA DÅ DET KOMMER FRAM EN TYP HAN ÄR SUR OCH SÄGER: LÅTEN PUSH-UP SKAPAR HAT

VÄRLDEN SOM DEN ÄR KAN DEN ALDRIG ÄNDRAS DÄRFÖR ÄR DET BRA MED HAT

/////////////
RIFF
/////////////

STICK

/////////////
RIFF
/////////////

JAG SÄGER: OM MAN INTE HATAR

0160

Nadie debe ser autorizado en [...]
lo que la naturaleza creó en ar[...]
racial. Tu más elevado propós[...]
ha de ser el de mantener dich[...]
hacia una humanidad mejor, n[...]
La pureza de la más elevada c[...]
es el requisito esencial para c[...]
evolución superior. (III. TEN FE EN[...]

Raza ⌐
0157

Så HÄR GJORDE VI SKIV[...]

I november 2000 hyrde vi en replokal vid Skogskyrkogården i Stockholm. Vi började göra nya låtar och vår nye medlem EnKilleTill skolades in. Vi började klockan 8 på mornarna och höll på till 16. Oftast började det med att någon hade en idé, kanske en ackordföljd eller ett riff, och så fyllde alla andra på med sina egna idéer. Musikaliskt ville vi röra oss i alla riktningar så vi döpte låtarna efter olika förebilder, tex Nick Drake (En Grej Som Hände För Elva År Sen), Jon Spencer (Ang. Hat), Bruce Springsteen (Bredäng Centrum) och Lou Reed (Jimi Tenor och Kennet Johnsson). Istället för att, som dom flesta andra band, härma sig själv, så kan man lika gärna härma alla andra, tänkte vi, för att få så stor spridning på låtarna som möjligt. Efter en månad hade vi 15 låtar som vi tyckte höll måttet. Låtarna hade i det här läget inga texter. Vi spelade in en demo i vardagsrummet hemma hos Den Nye i Stureby. Han hade köpt en dator med inspelningsprogrammet

ProTools. Jag gjorde blajtexter, bara för att ha nåt att sjunga. Första raderna på det som sen blev Kaj och jag gick tex "Om du vill bli nåt inom TV - Så ska du äta mycket äpplen - För det är allmänt känt att äpplen - Gör så att dina ögon griper tag" I januari 2001 så skickade vi demon till vår A&R Per Helin på MNW. Han gillade det och beställde tid i Gula Studion i Malmö åt oss. Nu skulle jag bara skriva texterna. Fast det var svårt att hinna med, speciellt eftersom jag våren 2001 var pappa-ledig. Jag försökte, men det blev helt enkelt inte bra, min son tog för mycket av min tid och energi. Dessutom turnerade vi en hel del, med Trumpeten och Tjuven på blås. Men vi åkte ner till Malmö i alla fall i omgångar och spelade in låtarna utan sång under våren och sommaren. Bröderna Jens och Petter Lindgård var producenter och ljudtekniker, precis som på förra skivan. EnKilleTill hade utvecklats till lika delar gitarrist och klaviaturist i

ban[...]
gita[...]
Teno[...]
med[...]
skriv[...]
sing[...]
bör[...]
förf[...]
Förs[...]
Förn[...]
Oss [...]
Med[...]
Jag [...]
Texte[...]
- Ber[...]
Berä[...]
Und[...]
Qua[...]
Till [...]
litegn[...]
ville [...]
efte[...]
mes[...]
hete[...]

0159

VII. PERFECCIONA A TUS PRÓJIMOS: (P[...]
intrínsecamente similar, parecido, igual,..[...]
Todos los hombres blancos son tus herm[...]
de que algunos no sean tan valientes o i[...]
Es tu deber como nacional-socialista info[...]
y alentarles el corazón con valentía. Muc[...]
han sido confundidos y embrutecidos, po[...]
corrupción de nuestra alma racial; tú no [...]
ni obcecarte, por su degenerada condició[...]
de limpiarlos y devolverlos a su familia ra[...]

Perfecció[...]
0161

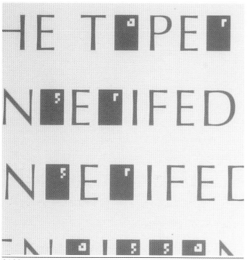

0162

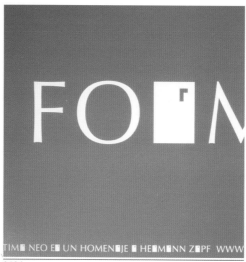

0164

0166

0163

Typog

0165

OPTIM■ NEO

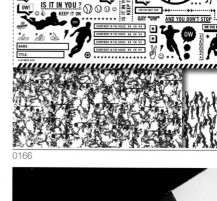

0167

0168
ALR Design
USA

0169
Ligalux GmbH
Germany

0170
Miriello Grafico, Inc.
USA

0171
Gouthier Design Inc.
USA

052/053
1000
Flyers +
leaflets

0168

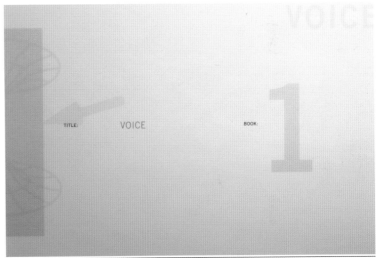

0170

0169

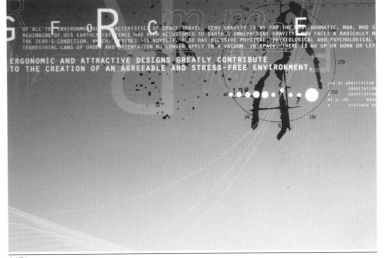

0171

0172
P22
USA

0173
P22
USA

0174
P22
USA

0175
P22
USA

0172

0174

0173

0175

0177

0179

0181

0178

0180

0182

83
0184
Segura Inc.
USA

0185
ALR Design
USA

0186
Harcus Design
Australia

056/057
1000 Flyers + leaflets

183

aling arms up, Biting nails, Finger sign, Flexing fing
ano fingers, Picking at skin, Poking, Popping knuc
aving, Inhaling, Exhaling, Gasping for breath, Kic
pping, Skipping, Jumping, Bending, Stooping, Step
ackward, Flexing ankles, Extending ankles, Tur
ot in, Turning foot out, Dragging foot, Shaking
amping feet, Tapping feet, Tripping, Toe cur
alking on toes, Banging table, Blowing on h
hewing on clothing, Flapping arms, Hitting self, Kis
and, Kissing others, Picking at lint, Pressing r
hincter, Pulling at clothes as if too tight, Scrat
elf, Shivering, Smelling fingers, Smelling obj
icking finger in throat, Twiddling thumb on n
wirling hair, Hunching over while walking, Whole
rking, Animal noises, Barking, Belching, Bur
lowing breath out, Coughing, Deep breathing, Grun
iccups, Hissing, Honking, Humming, Motor noise
ises, Screaming, Smacking lips, Sniffing, Sno

0185

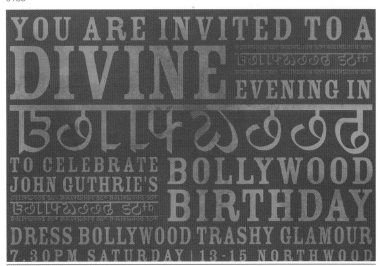

184

0186

Chapter 2.
Books + magazines.

0187
Starshot
Germany

0188
MAGMA [Büro für Gestaltung] & Christian Ernst
Germany

0190
Untitled
UK

0191
MAGMA [Büro für Gestaltung] & Christian Ernst
Germany

0192
Segura Inc.
USA

0193
Untitled
UK

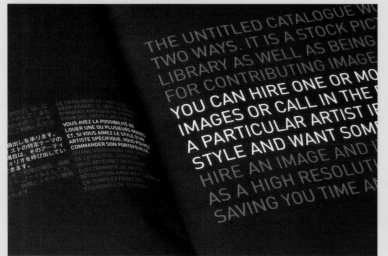

0190

0192

0191

0193

0195
MAGMA [Büro für Gestaltung]
& Christian Ernst
Germany

0196
Untitled
UK

062/063
1000
Books +
mags.

0197

0199

0201

0198

0200

0202

0203
Strichpunkt
Germany

0204
Strichpunkt
Germany

0205
Sweden Graphics
Sweden

0206
MAGMA [Büro für Gestaltung]
& Christian Ernst
Germany

0207
Ligalux GmbH
Germany

0208
emeryfrost
Australia

064/065 1000 Books + mags.

0203

IPO
CALYPSE NOW
EIN BÖRSENGANG IM // 04.07.
Y2K

0205

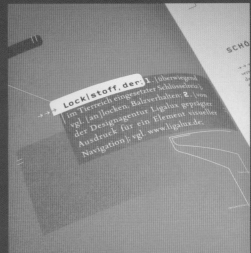

0207

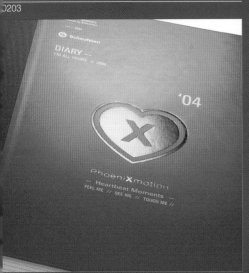

0204

0206

END

92>Writer's Shock
Toby Litt remembers the writer and educator
Malcolm Bradbury

95>Global Literary Calendar
Upcoming events around the world

96>Reviews
Authors on their own books; real kids on kids'
books; and Zembians on what to read now,
damn it

102>Big Philosophy, Big Talk
By Alexander Isak and Jan Söderqvist

112>Cartoon
By R. Crumb and Gavarni

115>Crossword: Crass Words
By Francis Heaney

116>Competition: Sex and Death
Who is the best qualified person to write on sex
and death? Tell Zembla publisher Simon Finch
and win a first edition classic novel

120>Lost Page
Never-before published pictures

MIDDLE – Fiction

38>Sanchakou
By Matthew Kneale

54>Under the Weather
By James Hopkins

66>The Marcus Van Heller Legend
An exclusive excerpt by John Stevenson

81>Sometimes the Daughter Says
the Things Her Mother Thinks
By Donna Daley-Clarke

87>Dr Mortimer's Observations
The problem with 'nice' people

0208

210
vo6
Brazil

0211
vo6
Brazil

0212
vo6
Brazil

0213
vo6
Brazil

066/067
1000
Books +
mags.

0210

0212

0211

0213

0214
The Design Dell
UK
↘

0215
MAGMA [Büro für Gestaltung] & Christian Ernst
Germany
↘↘

0216
**MAGMA [Büro für Gestaltung]
& Christian Ernst**
Germany
↘

0217
Strichpunkt
Germany
↘↘

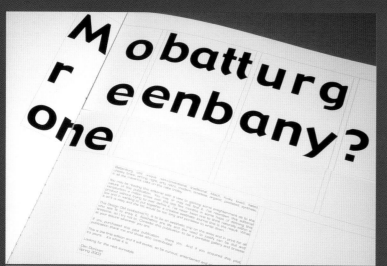

0214

0216

0215

0217

0218
MAGMA [Büro für Gestaltung]
Christian Ernst
Germany

0219
MAGMA [Büro für Gestaltung]
& Christian Ernst
Germany

0220
Jan Family
Denmark

0221
MAGMA [Büro für Gestaltung]
& Christian Ernst
Germany

068/069
1000
Books +
mags.

218

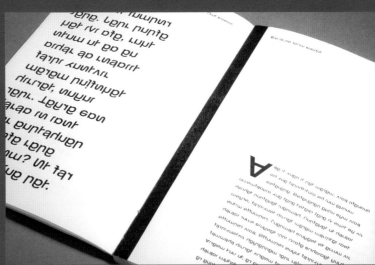

0220

219

0221

0222
Groothuis & Malsy
UK

0223
Johnson Banks
UK

0224
Duffy Singapore
Singapore

0222

0223

0224

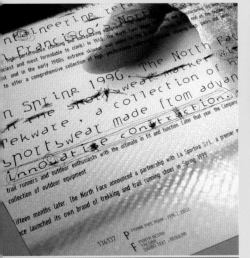

0225

0227

0229

0226

0228

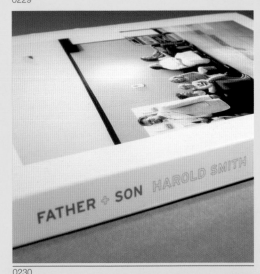

0230

0232
AGMA [Büro für Gestaltung]
Christian Ernst
Germany

0233
emeryfrost
Australia

0234
Segura Inc.
USA

0235
Strichpunkt
Germany

0236
MAGMA [Büro für Gestaltung]
& Christian Ernst
Germany

0237
Blackletter Design Inc.
Canada

072/073
1000
Books +
mags.

0232

0234

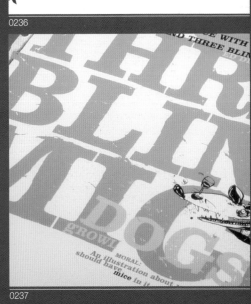

0236

0233

0235

0237

0238   0239
Yanek lontef   **Yanek lontef**
Israel   Israel

0240   0241
Yanek lontef   **Yanek lontef**
Israel   Israel

0242   0243
Yanek lontef   **Yanek lontef**
Israel   Israel

0238

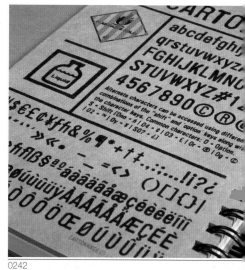

0240

0239

0241

0243

05_RENNRAD

STARTALK
GILBERTO SIMONI
EIN MODERNES MÄRCHEN

startalk

049

051

5/01   5/02

FOTO_KAI STUHT
ASSISTENT_RALF SCHUPP
INTERVIEW_KAI STUHT, ÜBERSETZUNG BEPPO HILFIKER
LOCATION_SPAIN
THANKS TO CANNONDALE/SAECO

0248
**MAGMA [Büro für Gestaltung]
& Christian Ernst**
Germany

0249
WilsonHarvey/Loewy
UK

0250
Mirko Ilić Corp.
USA

0251
WilsonHarvey/Loewy
UK

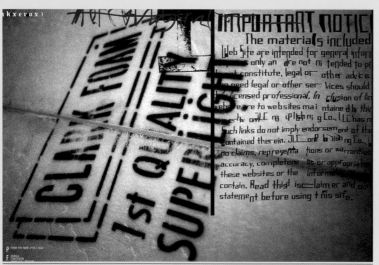

0248

0250

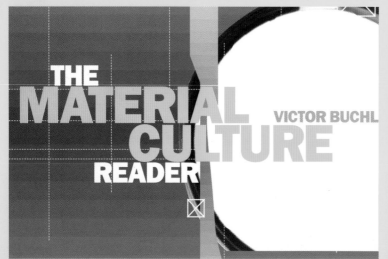

0249

0251

0253

0254

0255

0256

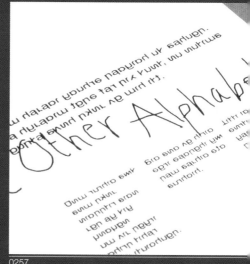

0257

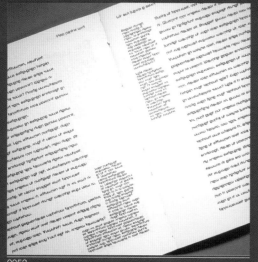

0258

0259
emeryfrost
Australia

0260
Strichpunkt
Germany

0261
emeryfrost
Australia

0262
emeryfrost
Australia

0263
Groothuis & Malsy
UK

0264
Plan-B Studio
UK

080/081
:1000
Books +
mags.

0259

BY TOBIAS HILL

ple things

Some people have a fear of water. Peter has a fear of snow. It has something to do with the definition of space, the way the sky is revealed, huge, plotted out in the helter-skelter course of snowflakes. it always occurs to him that the sky is much larger than he thought, a smaller than he ever imagined.

PHOTOGRAPHY: ALAN ROSS

0261

0263

0260

0262

0264

Contemporary
African Art and
Shifting Landscapes

Edited by
Gilane Tawadros and
Sarah Campbell

Fault Lines

0268
Blackletter Design Inc.
Canada

0269
Blackletter Design Inc.
Canada

0270
Blackletter Design Inc.
Canada

0271
Blackletter Design Inc.
Canada

0268

"Ooh-laa-laA"
Dixie makes us cheer
D is for "Dreamy"
D is for "Delectable"

0270

S is for "Sid"
serenading Sidney, grinning from ear t
S is for "Showtunes"
"I'm SEXY
FOR MY SKULL SEXY
OR MY SKULL SEXY
OOooH SASSY
2 SKULLY"

0269

C is not for "Cat"
is for spicy "Thai takeout"
T is for "Tonsils"
O is for "Operation"
see "Kurt"

0271

CRUNCHiE CRUNCH
CRUNCHCRA
CHOMPING COO-COO CORNS!!!
UMING CREAMY CORNY CORNS
ND CHEWING CHOO-CHOO CHEWY CUDS!!!
R NAME IS "CASSEROLE
CARRY ON LITTLE COWS
R is for "Rawhide!!!"

0272
Blackletter Design Inc.
Canada

0273
Blackletter Design Inc.
Canada

0274
Blackletter Design Inc.
Canada

084/085
1000
Books +
mags.

0273

Xenon 250 g/m² // 93lb cover

Testing the raw materials in the Scheufelen laboratory / Echantillons de pâtes à papier du laboratoire
de Scheufelen / Analisi sulle materie prime nei laboratori Scheufelen

>>> /

→ BRILLANTE NEBENWIRKUNGEN
→ VERTRAUEN IST GUT, KONTROLLE IST BESSER

Papierrohstoffproben aus dem Scheufelen Testlabor:

:PhoeniXmotion

→ MINDESTENS DREIMAL TÄGLICH!

morgens: KAOLIN AUS GEORGIA, USA
mittags: KREIDE AUS DEUTSCHLAND
abends: MARMOR AUS NORWEGEN

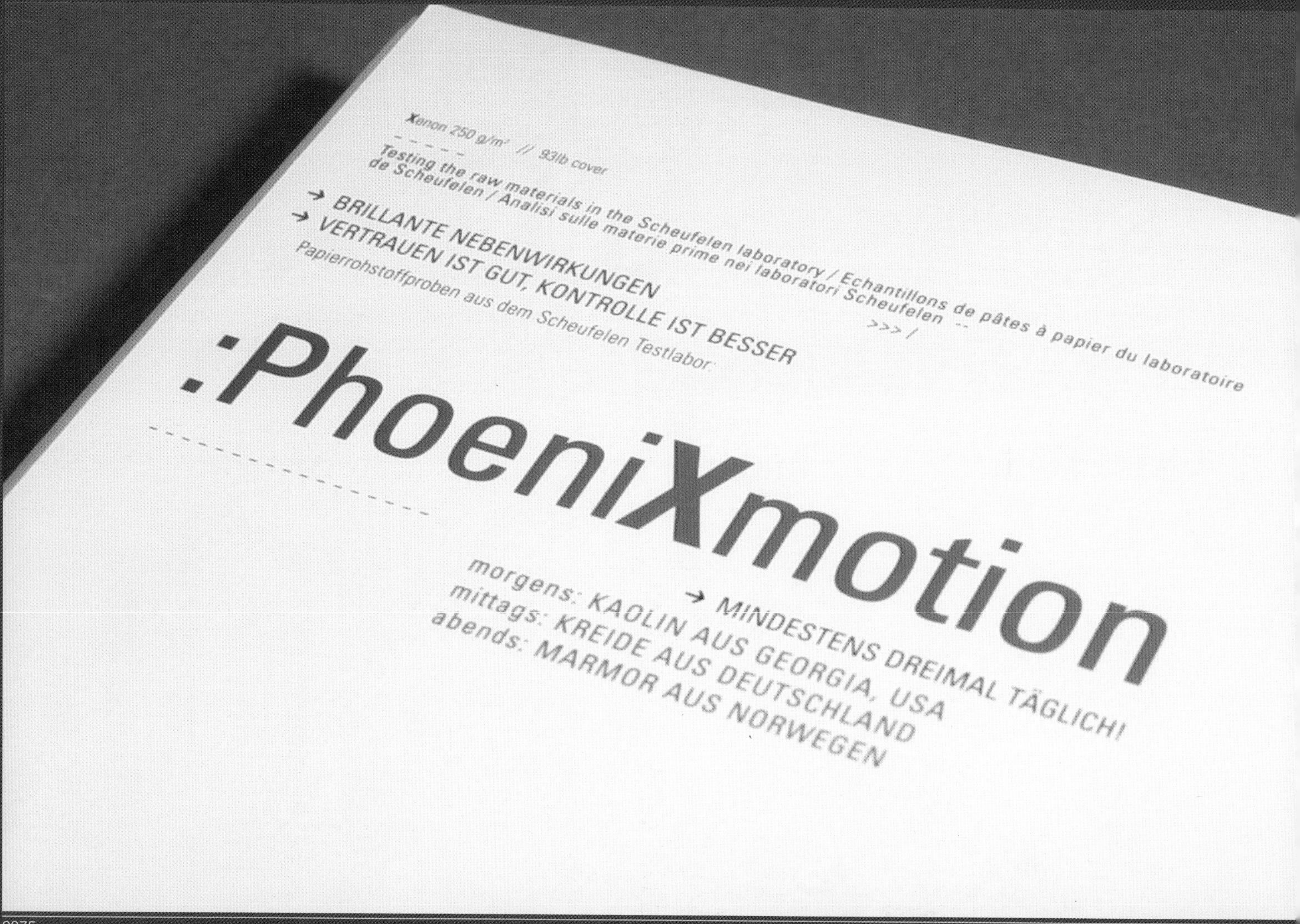

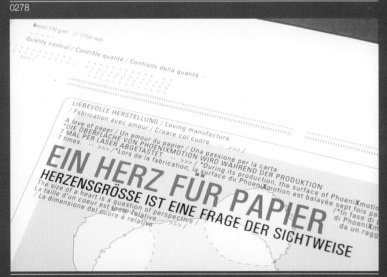

276

0277
The Family Design International
UK

0278
Kontour Design
USA

0279
Strichpunkt
Germany

086/067
1000
Books +
mags.

arshot
Germany

0280
Non-Format
UK

0281
Non-Format
UK

0282
Non-Format
UK

0283
Plan-B Studio
UK

RECESSIONAL

01: Opposite Corners
02: Shadow Traffic
03: Fare To Remember
04: Night On The Ocean
05: EuMix
06: Swing Moderate White
07: Installation Linoleum
08: Figures Like Tildes
09: Chill Rooms
10: Moving Platform
11: T.V.
12: Study In Scarlet
13: Pacific Gravity (Vocal Version)
14: More North Than Portland
15: Come Back Again

THE STATE OF SONG

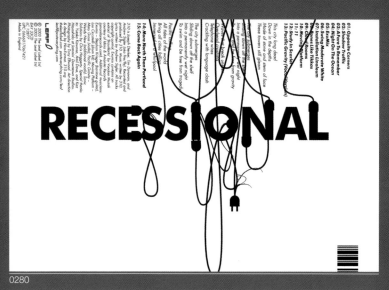

ANTI--ROCK CONSORTIUM

Although he's been a globally renowned artist for two decades, **Mike Kelley's** parallel career in music and sound art is a story rarely told. It is a tale that begins in Detroit with the post-Stooges punk noise insurgency of Destroy All Monsters, and winds up in Los Angeles via conceptual rock mythmaking with Tony Oursler in The Poetics, and collaborations with Sonic Youth, Scanner and Jean Baudrillard.
Words: Edwin Pouncey, Photos: Robert Gallagher

0.3 DAN BURTON DIVING XPERT

AN INTEREST IN EXTREME SPORTS CAN START EARLY FOR DAN BURTON IT ALL STARTED AT THE AGE OF FOUR, AND AS A CHILD HE BECAME AN EXCELLENT SKIER AND SKI RACER, MAKING REGULAR VISITS TO THE ALPS FOR RACING EVENTS WHEN HE WAS JUST 11 YEARS OLD

0.3 DAN BURTON

0284
Ian-B Studio
K

0285
MAGMA [Büro für Gestaltung] & Christian Ernst
Germany

0286
emeryfrost
Australia

0287
Non-Format
UK

XTREME SPORTS PHOTOGRAPH

INTRODUCTION

FUN WITH LISTS

Are you who you say you are?

BORN AGAIN
WILLIAM BURROUGHS'S
NAKED LUNCH

NAKED LUNCH
the restored text

william s. burroughs

DIE ERDE STIRBT NICHT VON SELBST. SIE
WIRD GETÖTET. UND DIE TÄTER HABEN
NAMEN UND-ADRESSEN.

UTAH PHILLIPS

THRIVING
BY ACCIDENT

0288
MAGMA [Büro für Gestaltung]
& Christian Ernst
Germany

0289
Stvarnik
Slovenia

0290
Mirko Ilić Corp.
USA

0288

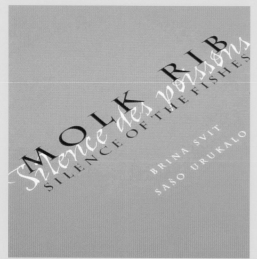

0289

0290

0291

0292
Stvarnik
Slovenia

0293
WilsonHarvey/Loewy
UK

0294
Stvarnik
Slovenia

0295
Stvarnik
Slovenia

0296
**MAGMA [Büro für Gestaltung]
& Christian Ernst**
Germany

090/091
1000
Books +
mags.

MAGMA [Büro für Gestaltung]
Christian Ernst
Germany

0291

0293

0295

0292

0294

0296

298 | 0299 | 0300 | 0301 | 0302 | 0303 | 092/093

an-B Studio | **Starshot**
Germany

Starshot
Germany | **Plan-B Studio**
UK

Cahan & Associates
USA | **Strichpunkt**
Germany

1000
Books +
mags.

298

0300

0302

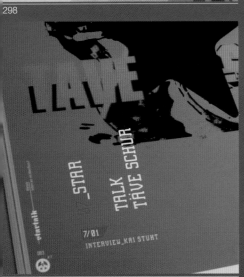

299

0301

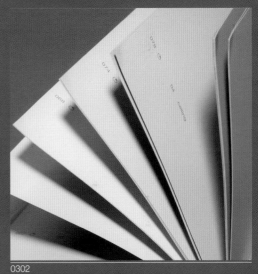

0303

0304	0305
WilsonHarvey/Loewy	**emeryfrost**
UK	Australia

0306	0307
Eggers & Diaper	**WilsonHarvey/Loewy**
Germany	UK

0308	0309
Thompson	**Stvarnik**
UK	Slovenia

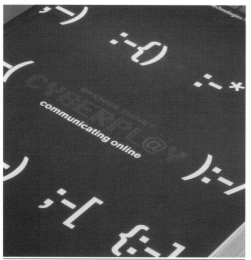

0304

0306

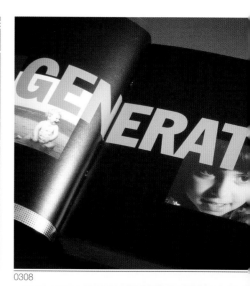

0308

0305

0307

0309

0310

0311

Ash Gibson
UK

0312

Stvarnik
Slovenia

0313

emeryfrost
Australia

094/095 | 1000
Books +
mags.

0310

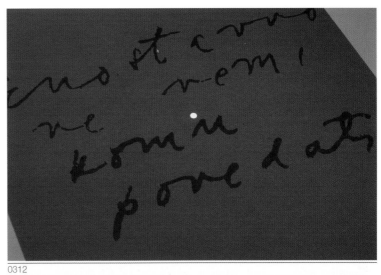

0312

0311

0313

0314
WilsonHarvey/Loewy
UK
↘

0315
WilsonHarvey/Loewy
UK
↘↘

0316
Aloof Design
UK
↘

0317
WilsonHarvey/Loewy
UK
↘↘

0314

0316

0315

0317

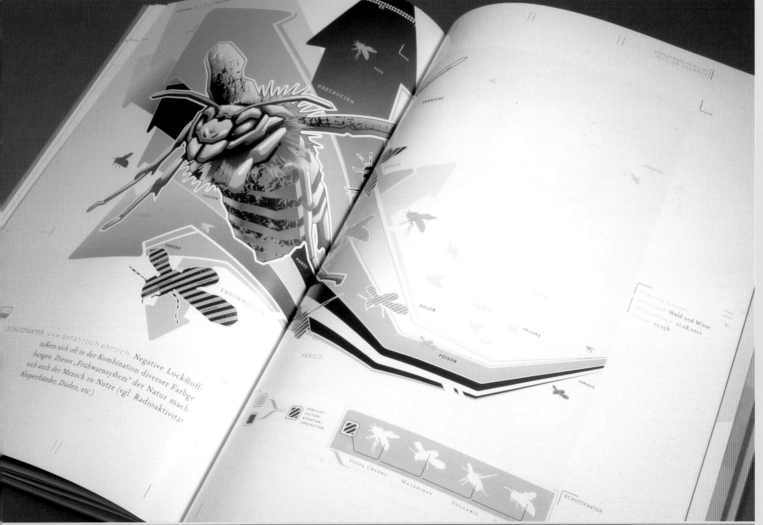

0319 **Strichpunkt** Germany ↘

0320 **Strichpunkt** Germany ↘↘

0321 **AdamsMorioka, Inc.** USA ↘

0322 **Strichpunkt** Germany ↘↘

0323 **The Design Dell** UK ↘

0324 **Ligalux GmbH** Germany ↘↘

heartbeat factor
WIE WAR DEIN TAG? /
BEWERTE IHN AUF EINER SKALA VON 1-5 // ⓧ ⓧ ⓧ ⓧ ⓧ //

heartbeat moments
MONAT FÜR MONAT / HEARTFACTS VON SCHEUFELEN /
ZUM SEHEN / FÜHLEN / NACHERLEBEN //

'04

→ PURE EMOTION IN PAPER

0319

ted a fac-
architects
d to the
between
ctice. An
and re-
cipline of
ral to the
This pub-
d for the
nvention
stitute of

0321

the substantial efforts of
SCI-Arc's faculty and former
students to contribute to
the built environment of Los
Angeles. *Projects range from
restaurants and boutiques
to museums, schools and
child care centers, demon-
strating the varied forms
of contemporary practice
that emerge from a need
to test ideas by building.*

0323

heartbeat
MOMENT #**09** ≙ HEARTFACT, NR 9

→ HEAVY WEIGHT

100 G	270 G	500 G	**2000 G**

1) NEUGEBORENES
2) ERWACHSENER
3) SPORTLER
4) **BEI LIEBESKUMMER**

0320

SIGNIFICANTLY
X-mm 170 g/m² // 1156 text

PhoeniXmotion comes 30 times per heartbeat* / PhoeniXmotion s'emploie 30 x le temps d'un battement d'un cœur* /
PhoeniXmotion viene 30 volte nell'arco di un battito cardiaco* ~

→ PAPIERAUSSTOSS
papier output // sortie du papier // rendimento della carta

PhoeniXmotion
KOMMT: 30x PRO
HERZSCHLAG*

0322

→ BEOBACHTUNG:

2%

der empfangenen
Informationen werde
verarbeitet.

0324

325
galux GmbH
many

0326
Ligalux GmbH
Germany
↘

0327
Ligalux GmbH
Germany
↘ ↘

098/099
1000
Books +
mags.

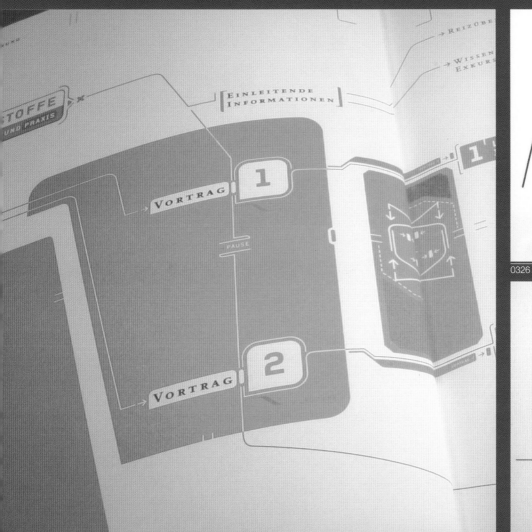

0326

0327

0328
Strichpunkt
Germany

0329
Strichpunkt
Germany

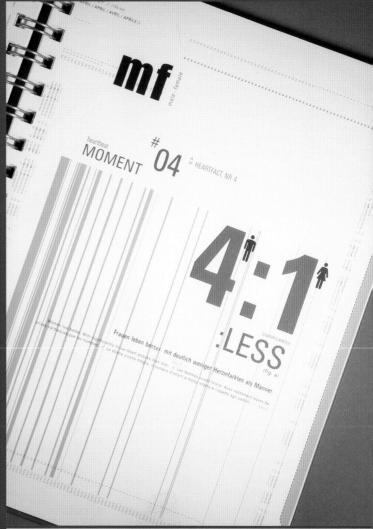

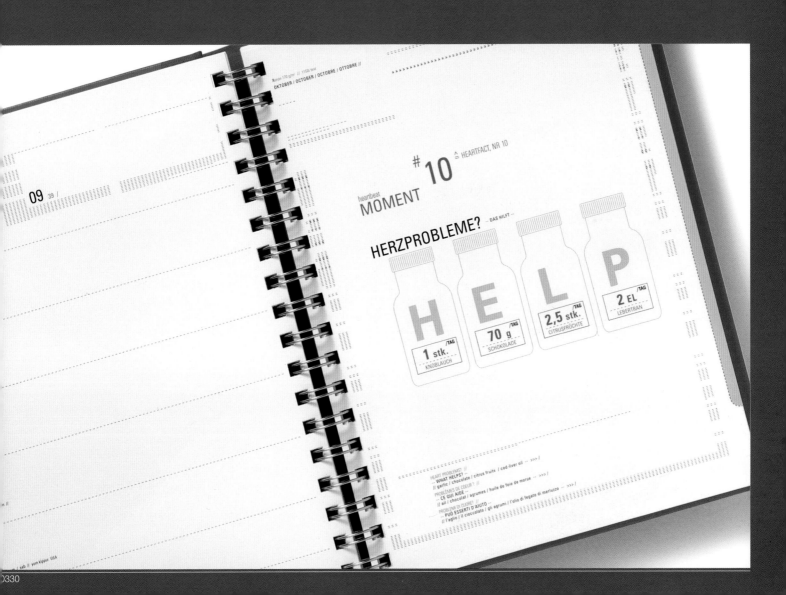

pocky

AMERICA VERA-ZAVALA
GLOBAL RÄTTVISA
ÄR MÖJLIG

Global rättvisa är möjlig är en unik bok. Den erbjuder nämligen två alternativa förklaringar till varför 1,2 miljarder av människorna i världen idag är extremt fattiga, vilka som har makten att förändra de rådande förhållandena och vad som krävs för att världen ska bli mer rättvis. Vänder du på boken finner du att det America Vera-Zavala, frontfigur i Attac och Ung Vänster, som redogör sin syn på världen.

som författare. Från det här hållet är det America Vera-Zavala,
ska bli mer rättvis. Vänder du på boken finner du att det
i världen idag är extremt fattiga, vilka som har makten att förändra de rådande förhållandena och vad som krävs för att världen
Global rättvisa är möjlig är en unik bok. Den erbjuder nämligen två alternativa förklaringar till varför 1,2 miljarder av människorna

CIRKAPRIS 69 KR (25% MOMS)
CIRKAPRIS 59 KR (6% MOMS)
ISBN 91-8-8420-86-8

pocky
9 789188 420862

JOHAN NORBERG
GLOBAL RÄTTVISA
ÄR MÖJLIG

Global rättvisa är möjlig är en unik bok. Den erbjuder nämligen två alternativa förklaringar till varför 1,2 miljarder av människorna i världen idag är extremt fattiga, vilka som har makten att förändra de rådande förhållandena och vad som krävs för att världen ska bli mer rättvis. Vänder du på boken finner du att America Vera-Zavala, frontfigur i Attac och Ung Vänster, står som författare. Från det här hållet är det Johan Norberg, liberal debattör verksam vid tankesmedjan Timbro, som redogör för sin syn på världen.

9 789188 420862

RIS 69 KR (25% MOMS)
RIS 59 KR (6% MOMS)
1-8-8420-86-8

pocky

0334
Ligalux GmbH
Germany

0335
Ligalux GmbH
Germany

0336
Ligalux GmbH
Germany

0337
Ligalux GmbH
Germany

0334

0336

0335

0337

338

galux GmbH
rmany

0339
Ligalux GmbH
Germany

0340
Ligalux GmbH
Germany

0.1.A EINFÜHRUNG
Nach DIN 28.12.1977–FORSCHUNGSNORM 22769 HH

THESE: Zuviele Lockstoffe führen zu
Kontrollverlust.

VERSUCHSAUFBAU: Ihre Wahrnehmung in einer x-beliebigen Großstadt
ihrer Wahl.

→ [REIZÜBERFLUTUNG HEUTE

→ [WISSENSCHAFTLICHER

BEOBACHTUNG.0.1.A
Nach DIN 899.699.0

[A]

ETZT:
LOCKSTOFF
IN THEORIE UND PR
LE
NEBENSTEHENDE

0341

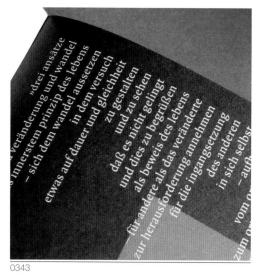

0343

0345

0342

0344

0346

47
ompson

0348
MAGMA [Büro für Gestaltung]
& Christian Ernst
Germany

0349
NB:Studio
UK

0350
Segura Inc.
USA

106/107
1000
Books +
mags.

347

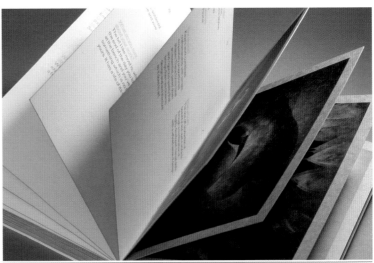

0349

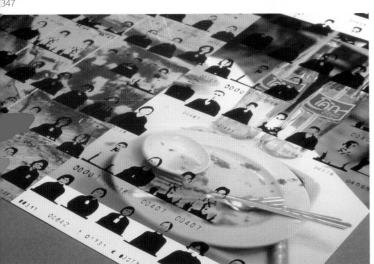

348

0350

0351
MAGMA [Büro für Gestaltung]
& Christian Ernst
Germany

0352
Non-Format
UK

0353
Non-Format
UK

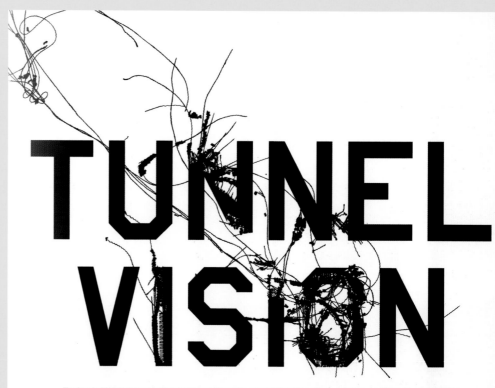

0351

0352

TUNNEL VISION

The Angels Of Light, formed in 1998 by Michael Gira as he emerged from Swans' long dark tunnel, might not be skullcrushing like a train coming the other way, but their songs are no less intense just because he's 'gone acoustic'. In this New York interview, Gira explains how his more melodic new material is still shaped by his formative experiences in punk, transgressive performance art and Glenn Branca's guitar orchestra, and explains how his Young God label has expanded to release artists such as Windsor For The Derby, Calla and outsider singer/songwriter Devendra Banhart.
Words: Alan Licht. Photos: Jo Ann Toy

0353

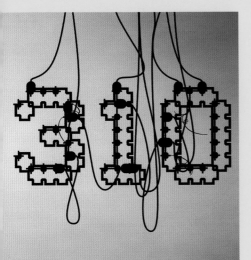

0354

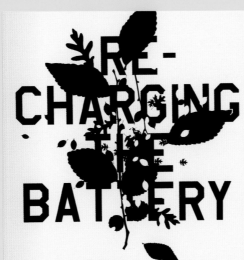

0356

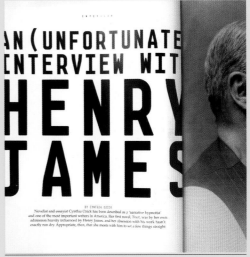

0358

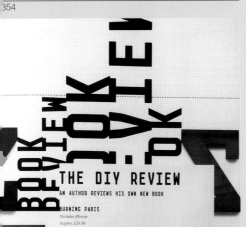

0355

0357

0359

61
e Design Dell

0362
WilsonHarvey/Loewy
UK
↘↘

0363
Groothuis & Malsy
UK
↘

0364
MAGMA [Büro für Gestaltung]
& Christian Ernst
Germany
↘↘

0365
MAGMA [Büro für Gestaltung]
& Christian Ernst
Germany
↘

0366
Ligalux GmbH
Germany
↘↘

110/111

1000
Books +
mags.

361

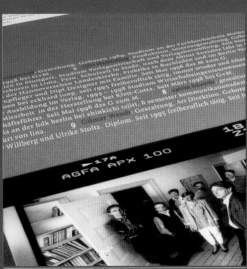

0363

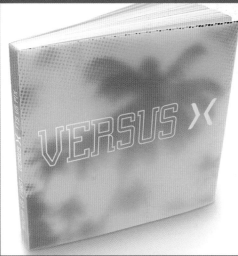

0365

362

0364

0366

Chapter 3.
Logos + stationery.

0367–0492

1888

Stationery

Logos

Brands

Compliment slips

Identities

Business cards

Letterheads

03 CAPOZZA
CA MA MD MI NH

unreal
able

brian eagle

creative director

12 Dyott St London WC

020 7379 8752 M 07787

eagle@unreal-uk.com

real-uk.com

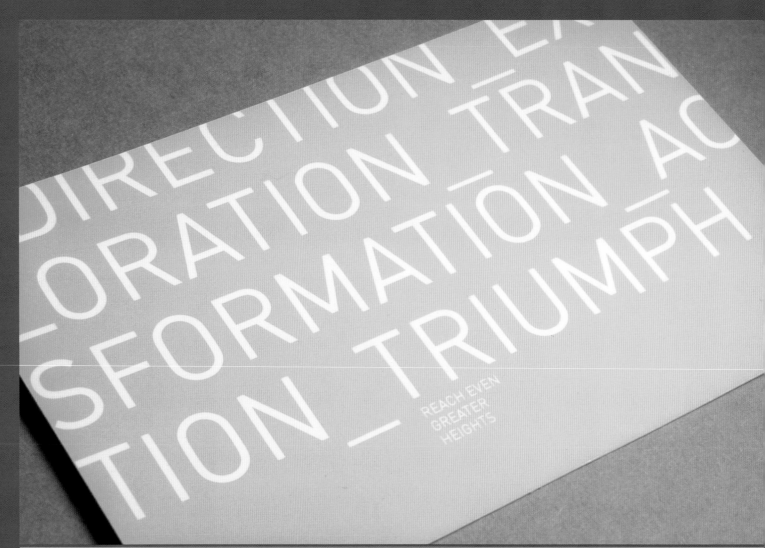

0368
e Miller's Company
SA

0369
Hartford Design, Inc.
USA

0370
Juicy Temples Creative
USA

0371
Danielle Foushée Design
USA

114/115 | 1000 Logos + stationery

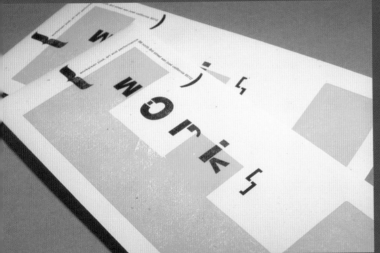

0368

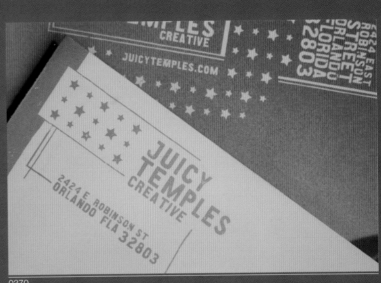

0370

0369

0371

0372

0374

0373

0375

76
.D
A

0377
Capsule
USA
↘

116/117
1000
Logos +
stationery

0378
Wolken Communica
USA

0379
Wolken Communica
USA

0380
KOREK Studio
Poland

MONOLITH

0378

0379

trans
FOR
mma

0380

31
0382
Family Design
Capaekel
ernational
UK

0383
0384
Segura Inc.
Si Scott
USA
UK

0385
0386
R&MAG Graphic Design
Marino A. Gallo
Italy
USA

118/119
1000
Logos +
Stationery

0381

0383

0385

OUTRA CLASSE
DE RÁDIO

0382

0384

0386

0387
Capsule
USA

0388
Capsule
USA

0390
**KearneyRocholl Corporate
Communications AG**
Germany

0391
**KearneyRocholl Corporate
Communications AG**
Germany

0392
**KearneyRocholl Corporate
Communications AG**
Germany

0393
**KearneyRocholl Corporate
Communications AG**
Germany

0394
**KearneyRocholl Corporate
Communications AG**
Germany

0395
**KearneyRocholl Corporate
Communications AG**
Germany

0390

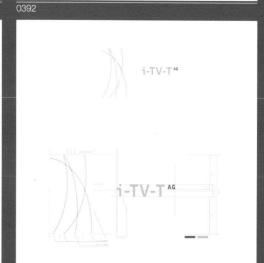

0392

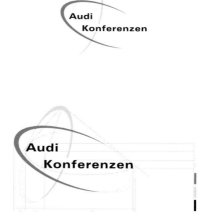

0394

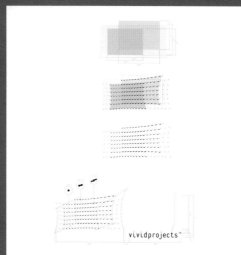

0391

0393

0395

KARMA

396

ARINYA ACCESSORIES

0398

JET

0400

O + V

397

OMVIVO

0399

wear®

0401

0402
Kontrapunkt
Slovenia

0403
Kontrapunkt
Slovenia

0404
Kontrapunkt
Slovenia

0405
WilsonHarvey/Loewy
UK

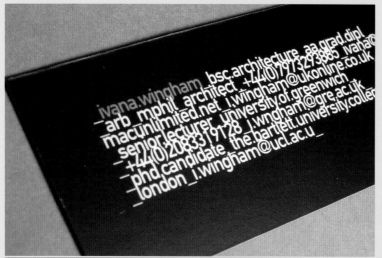

0402

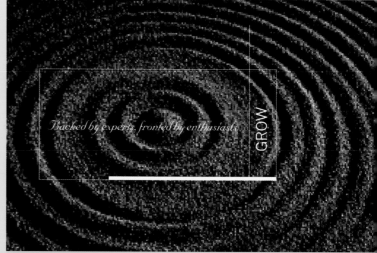

0404

0403

0405

06
uggie Ramadani Design Studio
nmark

0407
Unreal
UK

0408
Yanek Iontef
Israel

124/125
1000
Logos +
stationery

0407

0408

0409
Rose Design
UK

0410
Academy of Art University
USA

0411
Segura Inc.
USA

0412
Planet 10
USA

0409

0411

amelie
SHE WILL CHANGE YOUR LIFE

0410

0412

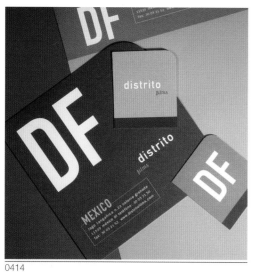

0414

0416

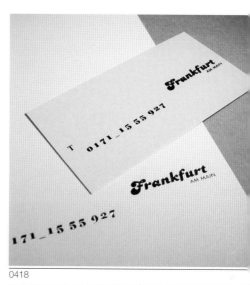

0418

0415

0417

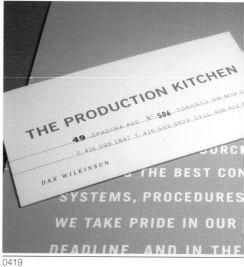

0419

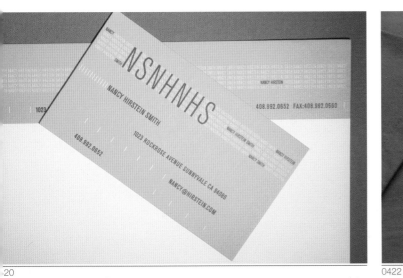

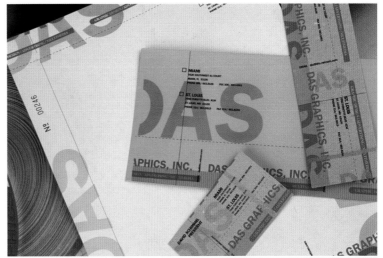

25   0426
cy Temples Creative   **Segura Inc.**
      USA

0427   0428
R&MAG Graphic Design   **Starshot**
Italy   Germany

0429   0430
Vrontikis Design Office   **Segura Inc.**
USA   USA

130/131

1000 Logos + Stationery

25

0427

0429

26

0428

0430

0431

0433

0435

0432

0434

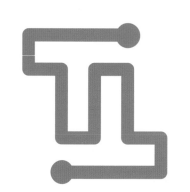

0436

37   0438 | 0439   0440 | 0441   0442 | 132/133

im Rashid Inc.   **Muggie Ramadani Design Studio**
       Denmark

The Family Design
International
UK

Ryan Burlinson
USA

Karim Rashid Inc.
USA

Joe Miller's Company
USA

1000 Logos + stationery

hairdesign

CAPOZZA
03 CAPOZZA REUNION
CA MA MD MI NH OR RI TX WA

(poetry center san josé)

0443
Blok Design
Mexico

0444
Kinetic Singapore
Singapore

0445
WilsonHarvey/Loewy
UK

0446
WilsonHarvey/Loewy
UK

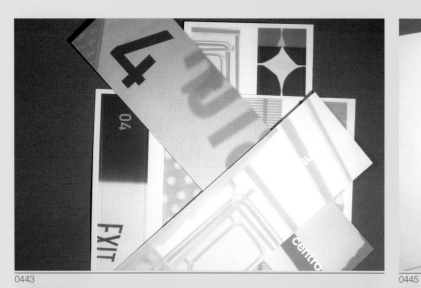

0443

0445

0444

0446

47

sonHarvey/Loewy

0448

Hartford Design, Inc.
USA

0449

Samen Weekende Ontwerpers
The Netherlands

134/135

1000
Logos +
Stationery

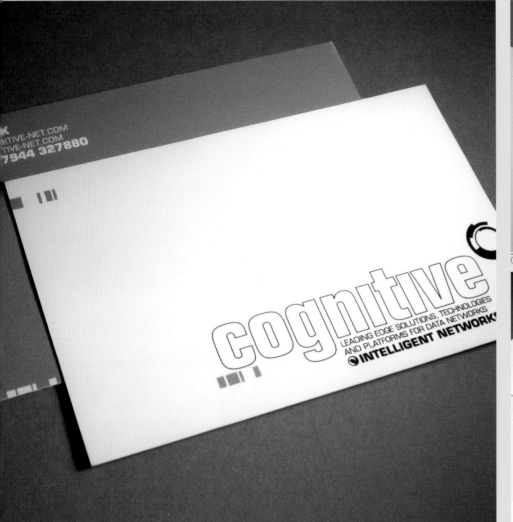

447

0448

0449

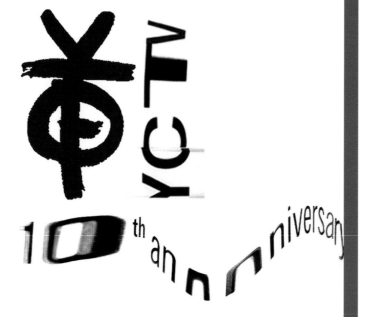

0453
Crush Design
UK
↘

0454
Crush Design
UK
↘↘

0455
Crush Design
UK
↘

0456
Crush Design
UK
↘↘

0453

CATATONIA

0455

0454

0456

57
Crush Design

0458
Crush Design
UK

0459
Crush Design
UK

0460
Crush Design
UK

138/139
:000
Logos +
stationery

0457

0459

0458

0460

Johann A. Gómez
USA

↘

62
Scott

0463
elliottyoung
UK
↘↘

0464
Marino A. Gallo
USA
↘

0465
elliottyoung
UK
↘↘

140/141
1000
Logos +
stationery

0466
**Muggie Ramadani
Design Studio**
Denmark

0467
**Muggie Ramadani
Design Studio**
Denmark

0468
**Muggie Ramadani
Design Studio**
Denmark

0466

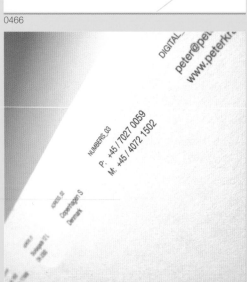

0467

0468

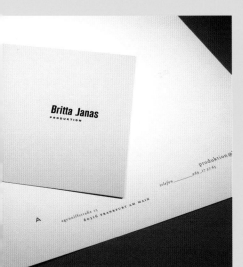

69

0471

0473

70

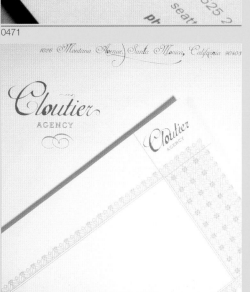

0472

0474

0475

0477

0476

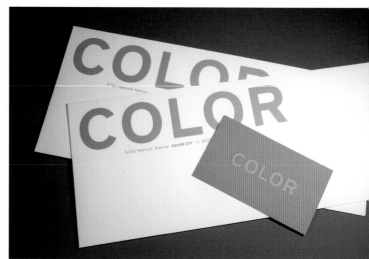

0478

79
k Design
xico

0480
**Muggie Ramadani
Design Studio**
Denmark

0481
Rinzen
Australia

144/145
1000
Logos +
Stationery

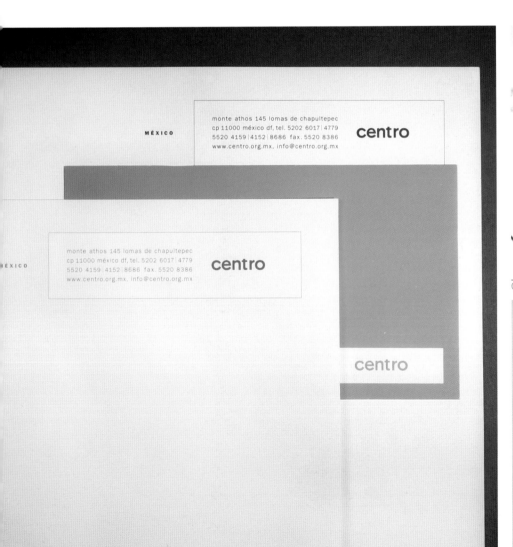

monte athos 145 lomas de chapultepec
cp 11000 méxico df, tel. 5202 6017 | 4779
5520 4159 | 4152 | 8686 fax. 5520 8386
www.centro.org.mx, info@centro.org.mx

MÉXICO

centro

0480

0481

0482
Blok Design
Mexico

0483
Dulude
Canada

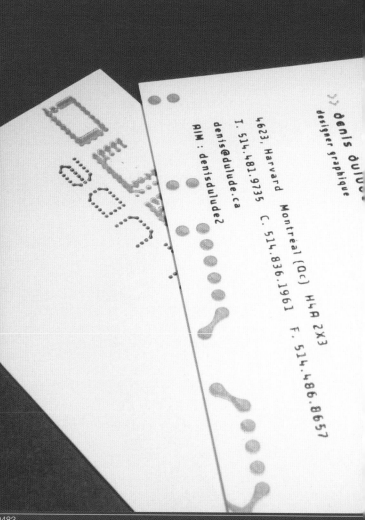

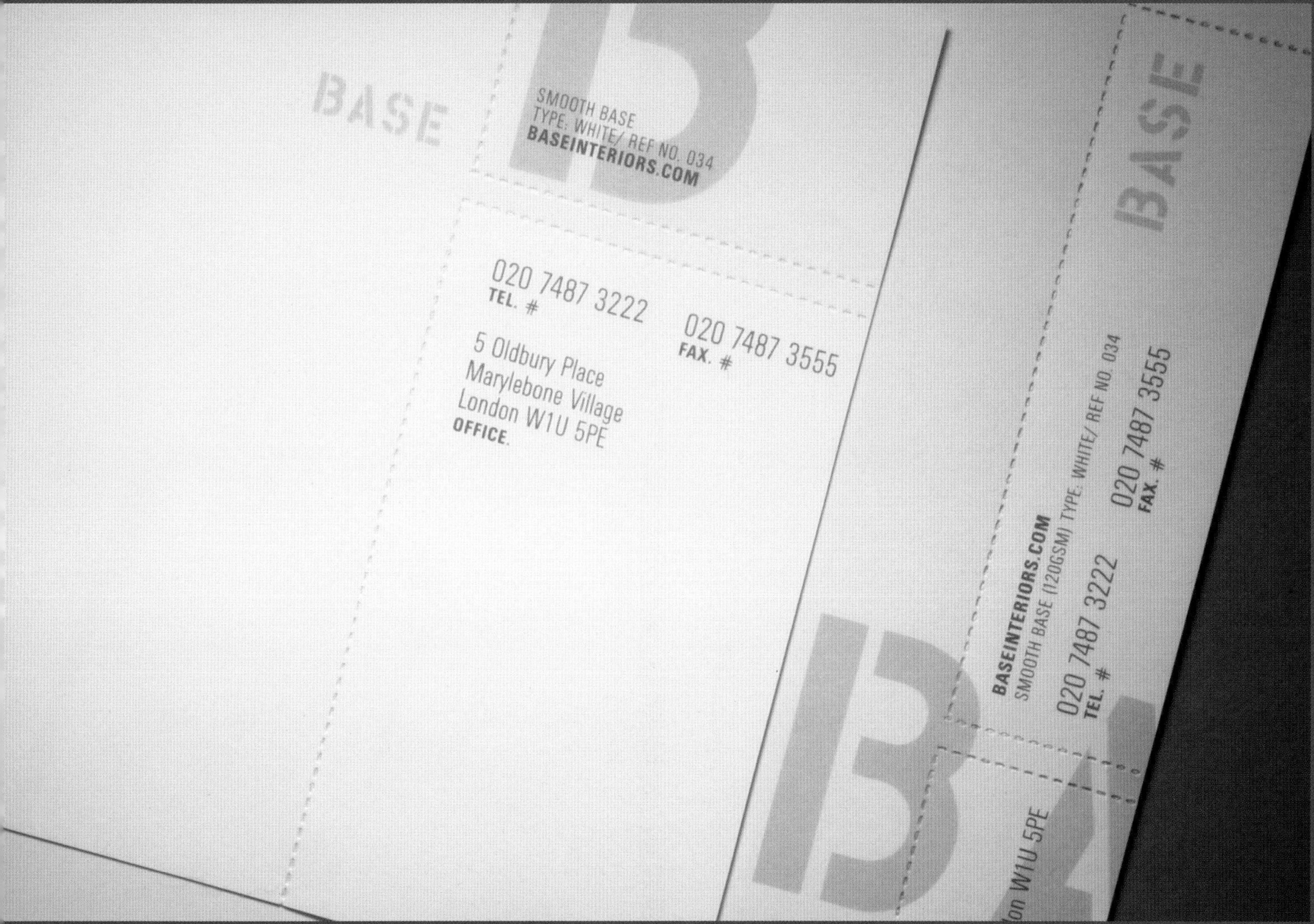

BASE

B

SMOOTH BASE
TYPE: WHITE/ REF NO. 034
BASEINTERIORS.COM

020 7487 3222
TEL. #

020 7487 3555
FAX. #

5 Oldbury Place
Marylebone Village
London W1U 5PE
OFFICE.

BASE

BASEINTERIORS.COM
SMOOTH BASE (120GSM) TYPE: WHITE/ REF NO. 034

020 7487 3555
FAX. #

020 7487 3222
TEL. #

B

on W1U 5PE

0485
Capaekel
UK
↘

0486
Crush Design
UK
↘↘

0487
SUMO
UK
↘

0488
Capaekel
UK
↘↘

0485

0486

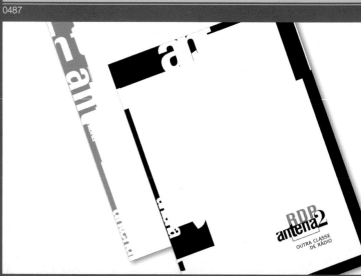

0487

0488

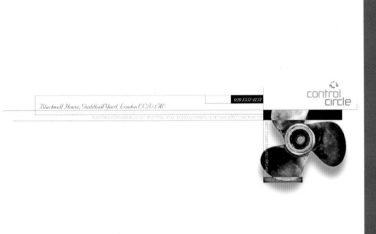

89

0491

490

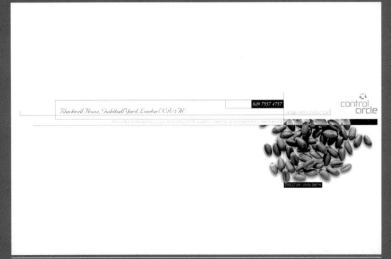

0492

Chapter 4.
Brochures.

Collateral

Annual reports

Product literature

Booklets

Pamphlets

Brochures

Folders

KINEMATIC

2002 Annual Report   Cause & Effect

S.A.W., INC. IS
ACCOMPLIS
MONTHS,
MOTIVA

Solutions At Work, Inc.   YR. 34

White papers

Mission Statement

ual Report

IT IS THE MISSION OF S.A.W., INC. TO PROVIDE
EMPLOYMENT, TRAINING, CAREER GROWTH, AND CUS
ORTS FOR PERSONS WITH MENTAL RETARD
EVELOPMENTAL DISABILITIES; TO EN
DENCE AND TO IMPROVE TH
RK AND PERSONAL LI

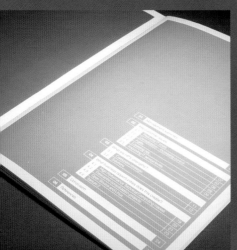

94

0496

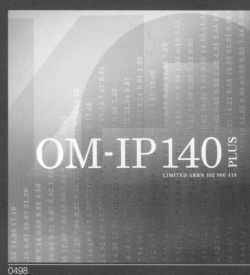

0498

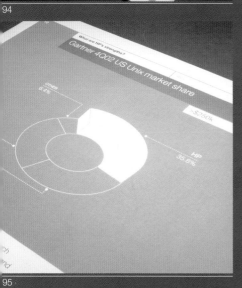

95

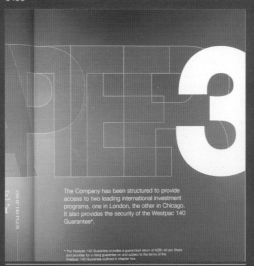

The Company has been structured to provide access to two leading international investment programs, one in London, the other in Chicago. It also provides the security of the Westpac 140 Guarantee*.

* The Westpac 140 Guarantee provides a guaranteed return of NZ$1.40 per Share and provides for a rising guarantee on and subject to the terms of the Westpac 140 Guarantee outlined in chapter two.

0497

0499

0500
Underware
The Netherlands

0501
Planet 10, Red Nose Studio
USA

0502
Planet 10, Red Nose Studio
USA

0503
Anna B. Design
Germany

0500

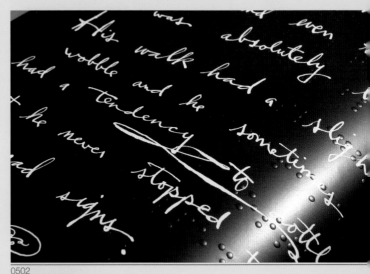

0502

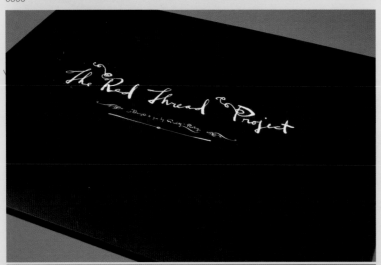

0501

0503

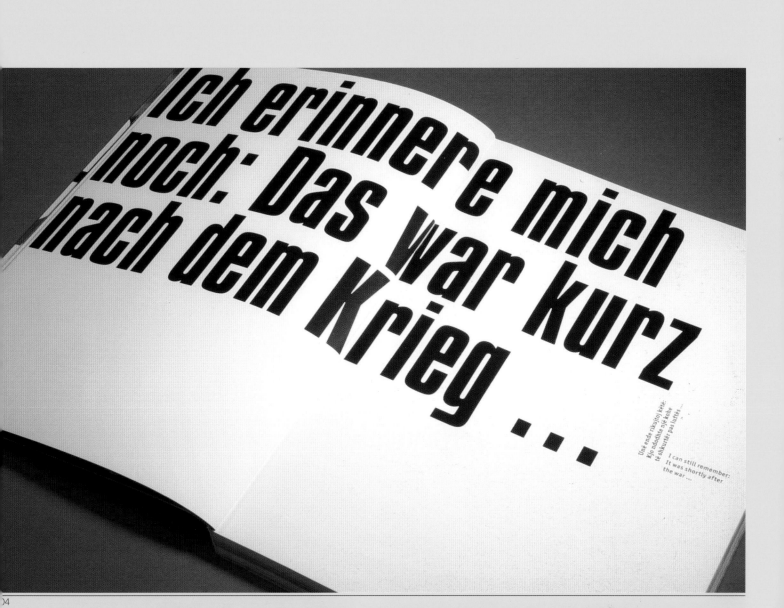

Ich erinnere mich noch: Das war kurz nach dem Krieg ...

Une ende rikujlaj kete:
Kjo ndodhte pjk kohe
te shkurtt pas luftes ...

I can still remember:
It was shortly after
the war ...

0505

0507

0509

0506

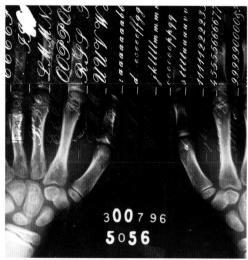

0508

0510

0511

0513

0512

0514

0515
Simon & Goetz Design
Germany

0516
Simon & Goetz Design
Germany

0517
A2-GRAPHICS/SW/HK
UK

0518
Simon & Goetz Design
Germany

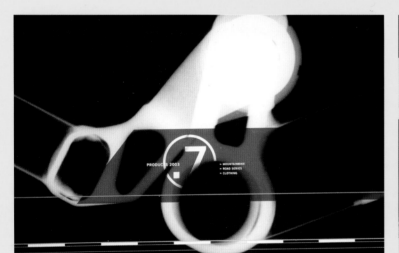

0515

0517

0516

0518

on & Goetz Design
many

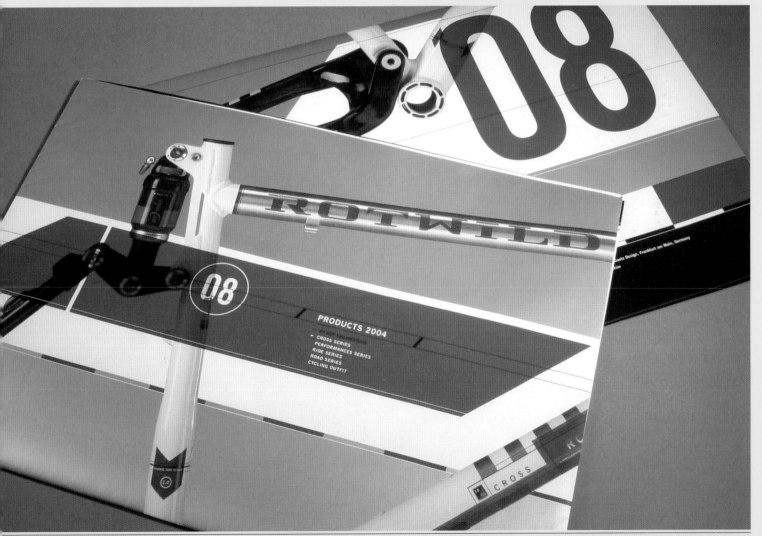

0520

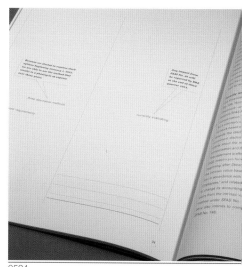

0522

0524

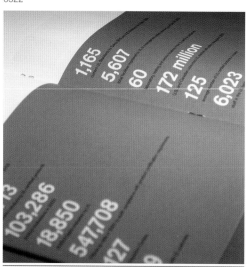

0521

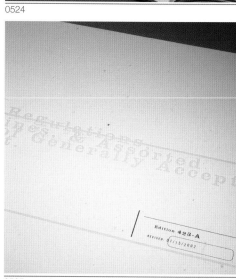

0523

0525

26 | 0527
...tford Design, Inc. | **WilsonHarvey/Loewy**
...A | UK

0528 | 0529
WilsonHarvey/Loewy | **Joe Miller's Company**
UK | USA

160/161
1000 Brochures

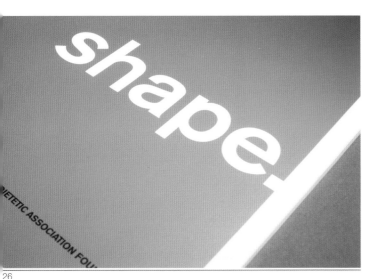

26

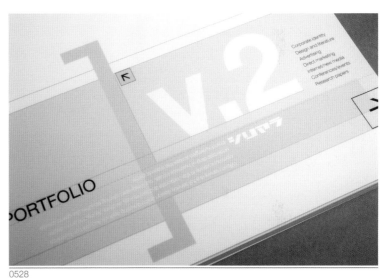

0528

27

0529

Hartford Design, Inc.
USA

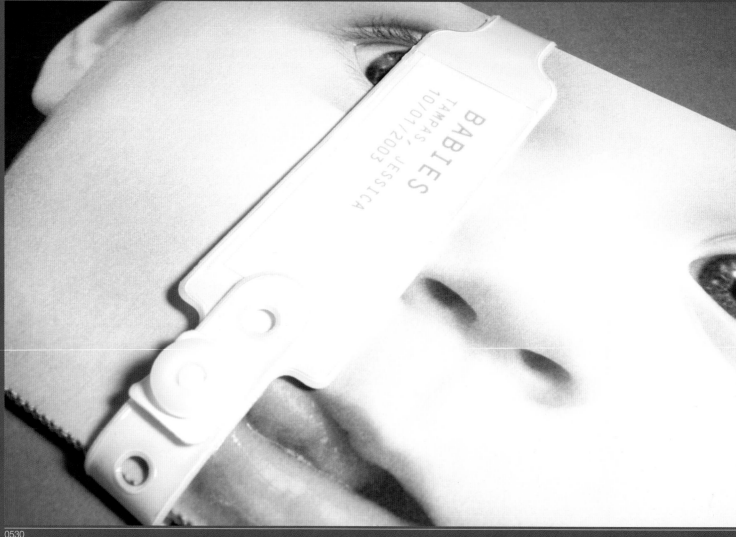

BABIES
TAMPAS
10/01/2003 JESSICA

0531

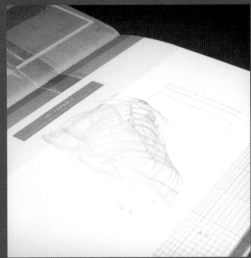

0533

For more than fifty years we have been building where we are the world's leading

manufacturers the widest selection of pharmaceutical, surgical, and consumer products for the eye.

0535

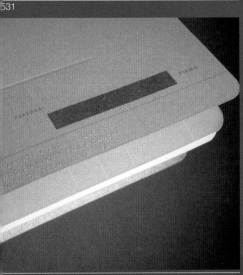

0532

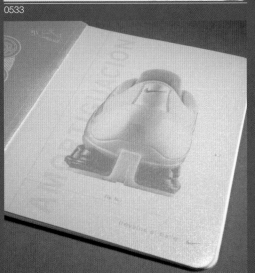

0534

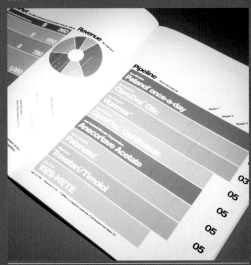

0536

0537
The Moral Animals/Form Fünf
Germany

0538
The Moral Animals/Form Fünf
Germany

0539
The Moral Animals/Form Fünf
Germany

0540
The Moral Animals/Form Fünf
Germany

0537

0539

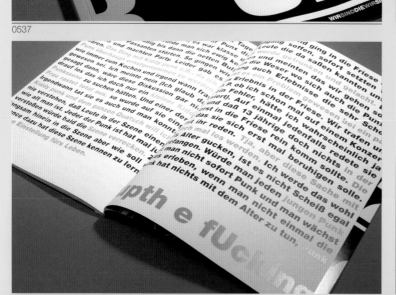

0538

0540

641
vision+
rmany

0542
Envision+
Germany

0543
Envision+
Germany

164/165
1000
Brochures

nose
food
native

and practices of peripheral populations. On the one hand – abstracted and unified in the imagination – they condense into a monstrous transcendent power: **the market**, the Thing from Outside, whose inexplicable and unpredictable 'forces' surreptitiously dominate the earth. On the other, they are hazily integrated into a wistful orientalism, as exotic tourist attractions (foreign bazaars and souks), or as anomalous pockets of immigrant eccentricity.

There is nothing arbitrary about this construction which constitutes a simultaneous – if fractured – response both to the autonomous or 'demonic' agency of emergent commercial singularities, and to their intense alliance with the periphery (with edges, outer limits, eccentricity, and marginality). Traders have always operated at the edges, and insofar as true markets still exist in the West they are primarily produced and supported by peripheral populations, amongst whom recent immigrants have a particularly crucial role.

markets emerge wherever the periphery cuts through a culture, as a spontaneous quence of disrupted centralism, unconstrained communication, and positive isation.

btedly a sense in which the repulsive forces of the metropolitan whatever disturbs them to the edges, but there is also a sense everywhere.

t: nick land and anna greenspan. n.land@inthepark.net,
a.greenspan@inthepark.net / p: martine bruno,
m.bruno@inthepark.net

DOWN

abhair gnó
talking business

0544
Dulude
Canada
↘

0545
Dulude
Canada
↘ ↘

0546
Dulude
Canada
↘

0547
Dulude
Canada
↘ ↘

0548
Dulude
Canada
↘

0549
Dulude
Canada
↘ ↘

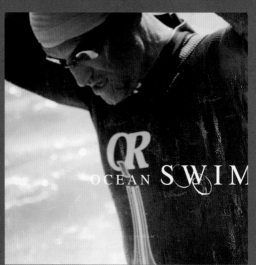

0544

0546

0545

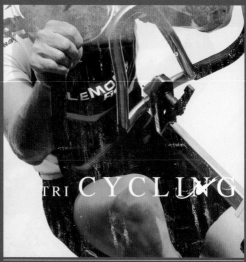

0547

0548

0549

50 0551
lude **Dulude**
ada Canada

0552 0553
Dulude **Dulude**
Canada Canada

0554 0555
Dulude **Dulude**
Canada Canada

166/167
1000
Brochures

0550

0552

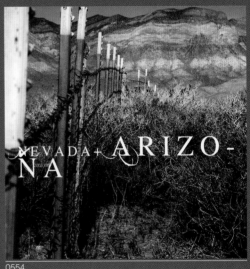

0554

551

0553

0555

0556
Untitled
UK
↘

0557
Untitled
UK
↘ ↘

0558
Untitled
UK
↘

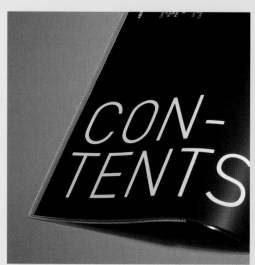

0556

0557

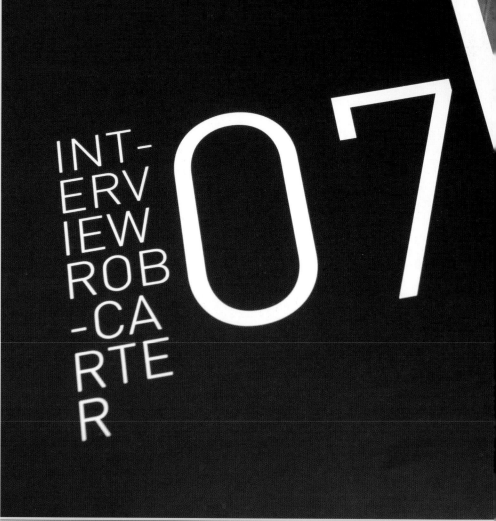

0558

59 | 0560
han & Associates | Cahan & Associates
 | USA
↘↘

0561 | 0562
Cahan & Associates | Cahan & Associates
USA | USA
↘ | ↘↘

0563 | 0564
Cahan & Associates | Untitled
USA | UK
↘ | ↘↘

168/169
1000 Brochures

59

0561

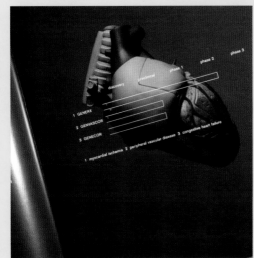

0563

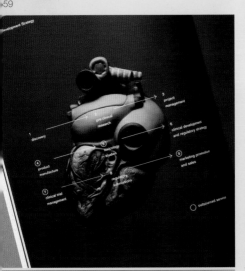

60

0562

0564

66

0567
Hornall Anderson Design Works, Inc.
USA
↘↘

0568
Hornall Anderson Design Works, Inc.
USA
↓

0569
Hornall Anderson Design Works, Inc.
USA
↓

170/171
1000
Brochures

66

0568

67

0569

0570
vo6
Brazil

0571
vo6
Brazil

0572
vo6
Brazil

0573
vo6
Brazil

0570

0572

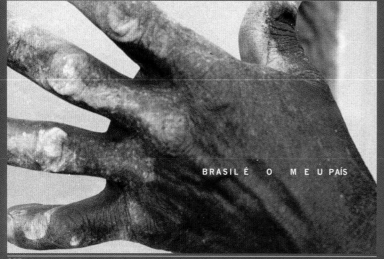

BRASIL É O MEU PAÍS

0571

0573

74 0575
vo6
Brazil

0576 0577 172/173
vo6 vo6 1000
Brazil Brazil Brochures

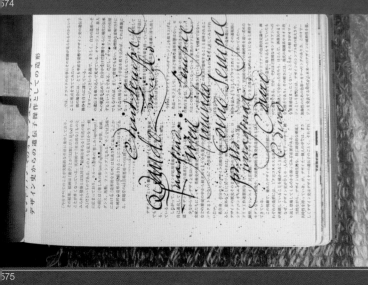

55°57'N 3°10'W
57
Dynamic Earth / Edinburgh

55°46'N 2°43'W
04
Seabird Centre / North Berwick

Bass Rock, the world's largest single rock geometry, is largely unobserved and rarely visited – apart from its thousands of feathered inhabitants. Visitors can now catch an intimate glimpse of the lives of North Atlantic Gannets and other seabirds, as cameras relay live pictures back to the Scottish Seabird Centre at North Berwick.

55°51'N 4°17'W
58
Hampden Park / Glasgow

All Regions
06
Beacons across the land

All Regions
48
TYX Talent & Skills 2000

All Regions
46
Sleeping in the Millennium

54°58'N 1°36'W
40
Centre for Life/Newcastle

Science and biotechnology, research and education, entertainment and ethics are brought together at the International Centre for Life in Newcastle. Exhibitions and lectures examine where life came from, how it works and what it means, and 'Superlab' offers an education resource for children of all ages. With laboratory spaces for schools as well as scientists, it opens the genetic debate to everyone.

54°55'N 1°09'W
09
Turning the Tide / Durham coast

54°35'N 1°14'W
16
Project SIX07/Teesside

All Regions
59
Cycle Network Artworks

54°59'N 2°36'W
22
Gateshead Millennium Bridge

All Regions
44
Year of the Artist

53°29'N 2°18'W
20
The Lowry/Salford

Salford Quays – at the heart of Manchester's waterways – plays host to The Lowry, a powerhouse for the performing and visual arts. Home to the world's largest collection of work by local artist LS Lowry, the centre also boasts exhibition spaces for visiting collections, plus two theatres.

53°32'N 2°18'W
10
National Foundation / Merseyside

All Regions
21
Millennium Greens

53°58'N 1°05'W
44
Mystery Plays / York Minster

53°30'N 2°58'W
24
Trans Pennine Trail

53°25'N 1°28'W
15
Earth Centre/Doncaster

53°00'N 2°11'W
17
cinema2a / Stoke-on-Trent

52°28'N 1°54'W
03
Towns Walkway / New Wills

52°29'N 1°52'W
35
Millennium Point / Birmingham

53°08'N 4°16'W
06
Rheilffordd Eryri / Snowdonia

After decades of neglect, a 14km section of the Welsh Highland Railway is being reconstructed, running from Caernarfon to Porthmadog. Due for completion in 2005, steam and diesel locomotives will climb through the Snowdonia National Park, offering passengers breathtaking views.

51°29'N 3°10'W
47
Canolfan Mileniwm/Cardiff

Providing a focus for Welsh culture, identity and talent is the Wales Millennium Centre on the Cardiff Bay waterfront. Musicals, opera and dance will be staged in a remarkable building forged from indigenous materials – including slate blocks from North Wales and fossilized tree ferns from the coal measures of South Wales.

51°28'N 2°36'W
33
Wildscreen at Bristol

Wildscreen-at-Bristol harnesses up-to-date computer and video technology to explain our natural world. A walk-through botanical house with free-flying birds and butterflies and a giant IMAX cinema enable visitors to watch nature on an incredible scale. Wildscreen's ARKive – a digital zoo – is a globally-accessible computerized library of wildlife films, photographs and sound recordings.

All Regions
42
Church Floodlighting

52°45'N 0°43'E
34
Norfolk and Norwich Project

52°14'N 0°43'E
41
St Edmundsbury Cathedral

For nearly 1000 years the site of the cathedral in Bury St Edmunds, Suffolk, has been a place of worship and pilgrimage. The construction of today's cathedral was started in 1503, yet remained unfinished, and the current project focuses on the completion of the North Transept, the Cloisters and the dramatic Central Tower.

52°30'N 0°05'E
02
National Space Centre / Leicester

51°30'N 0°07'W
01
Tate Modern / London

51°22'N 0°12'W
08
Lighting Croydon's skyline

51°00'N 0°00'
31
Millennium Seed Bank / Ardingly

51°32'N 0°02'W
23
Mile End Park / London

The redevelopment of Mile End Park in London's East End has been achieved through active cooperation with local residents. Community planning sessions highlighted the need for recreational facilities combined with environmental initiatives, and features include a swimming pool and athletics track, plus ecology and children's centres, gallery spaces, cafes and a concert stadium.

51°29'N 0°12'W
54
Web of Life / London Zoo

51°30'N 0°2'W
37
Body / The Dome

51°22'N 2°21'W
39
Bath Spa

50°48'N 1°06'W
12
Portsmouth Harbour

This historic maritime centre is being given a new waterfront. At the heart of the development is the impressive sail-like structure of the 165m Spinnaker Tower which will provide visitors with an unparalleled view of the Mary Rose and HMS Victory – potent reminders of the port's seafaring history.

54°35'N 5°42'W
13
ECOS/Ballymena

The ECOS project in Ballymena puts sustainability and biodiversity into action, with natural habitats developed to increase the number and diversity of plant and animal species in the area. The main building uses solar panels, wind turbines and renewable fuels for its energy requirements, while reed beds act as a natural filtration system to purify waste water.

54°12'N 6°41'W
43
St Patrick Centre / Downpatrick

All Regions
25
Strangford Stone / Killyleagh

50°20'N 4°42'W
30
Eden Project/St Austell

Visitors to the Eden Project in Cornwall have the opportunity to experience some of the world's most dramatic and useful plants at first hand, with two 60m-high 'biomes' (greenhouses) exhibiting plants from four climates – rainforest, mediterranean, desert and temperate. The project targets the relationship between people, plants and resources – and how this must be managed to improve sustainability.

51°34'N 2°59'W
11
Parc Arfordirol / Llanelli coast

All Regions
29
Years For The Millennium

All Regions
28
Groundwork's Changing Places

79 | 0580 | 0581 | 0582 | 0583 | 0584 | 174/175

pa Pearce Design, ndon

Lippa Pearce Design, London
UK

Lippa Pearce Design, London
UK

Lippa Pearce Design, London
UK

Lippa Pearce Design, London
UK

Lippa Pearce Design, London
UK

1000 Brochures

579

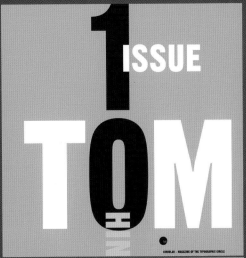

0581

0583

580

0582

0584

0585
Lippa Pearce Design,
London
UK

0586
Guru Design
Denmark

0587
Guru Design
Denmark

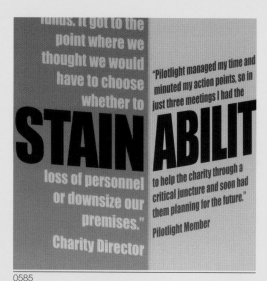

0585

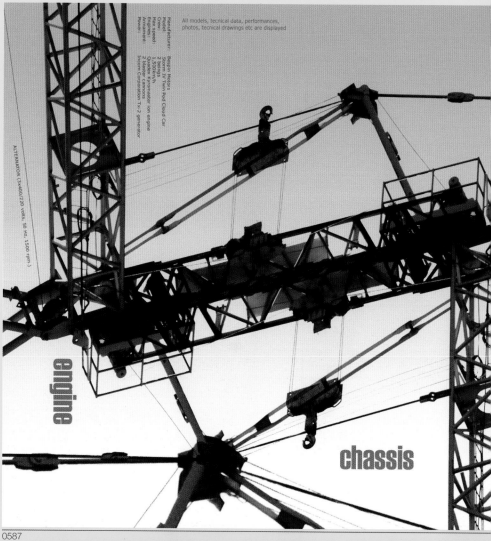

0586

0587

88
tford Design, Inc.
A

0589
Guru Design
Denmark

0590
Metal
USA

176/177
1000 Brochures

0589

0591	0592	0593
Cahan & Associates	**Enspace, Inc.**	**Enspace, Inc.**
USA	USA	USA

↘ ↘↘ ↘

0591

0592

0593

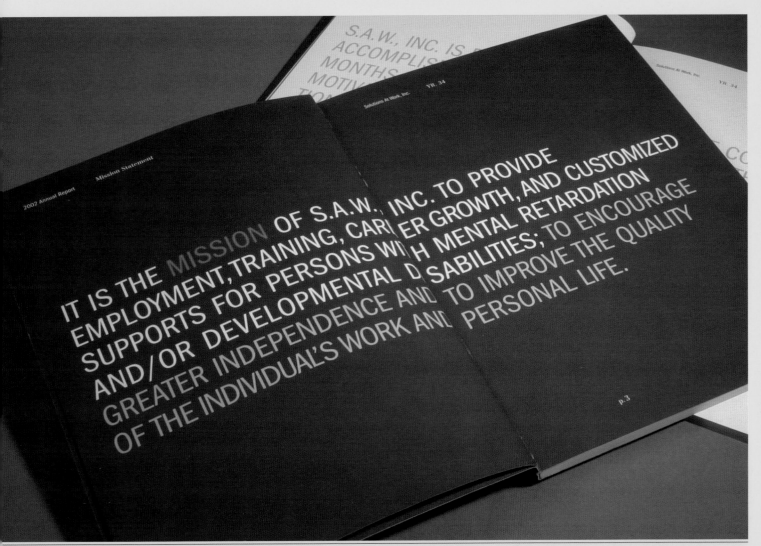

Neutro-
penia

Optimized
G-CSF
for the treatment
of neutropenia

Neutropenia is a severe decrease in neutrophil cell counts in the blood. Neutrophils are a specific type of blood cell that play an important role in the human body's defense against bacterial infections. Neutropenia is a common side effect from chemotherapeutic treatments of many forms of cancer, including breast cancer, lung cancer, lymphomas and leukemias. Neutropenic patients contract bacterial infections easily and often, some of which can be severe and life-threatening. Further, neutropenic patients may receive reduced or delayed chemotherapy treatment, which can result in disease progression.

Maxy
Optim
Maxy-

Indication
Neutropen

Current Mark
$2.0B

First Generation
Neupogen®

Second Generation
Neulasta®

96
GRAPHICS/SW/HK

0597
Bruketa & Zinić
Croatia
↘↘

0598
A2-GRAPHICS/SW/HK
UK
↘

0599
Bruketa & Zinić
Croatia
↘↘

180/181
:1000
Brochures

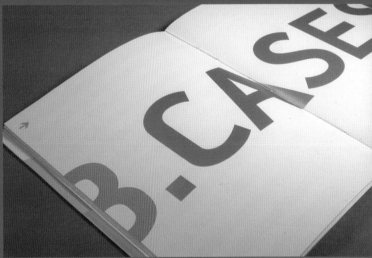

0600
Rose Design
UK
↘

0601
Rose Design
UK
↘↘

0602
Rose Design
UK
↘

0603
Anna B. Design
Germany
↘↘

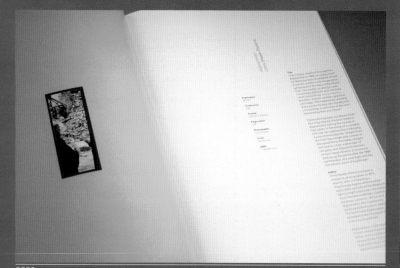

0600

Cultural Ties
Edited by Kapil Jariwala

Cover price
£40

Format
220mm x 120mm

Page extent
176

Photography
120 colour

Cover
Hardcover/silk-bound

ISBN
1 903391 08 3

0602

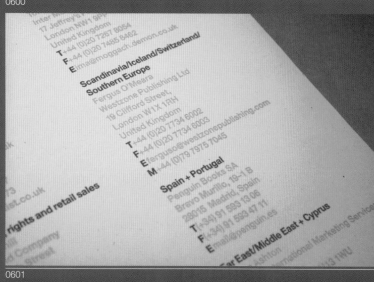

0601

0603

04 | 0605
yx Design | Blue River
UK

0606 | 0607 | 182/183
Twelve: Ten | Twelve: Ten | 1000
UK | UK | Brochures

↘↘ | ↘↘ | ↘↘

0604

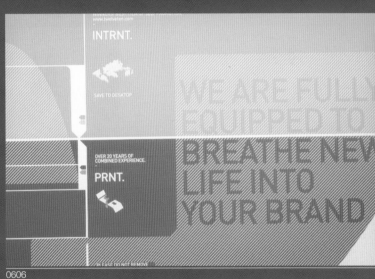

0606

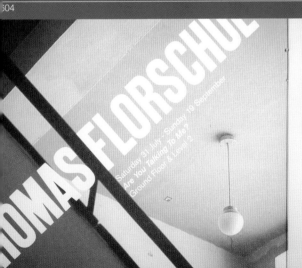

0605

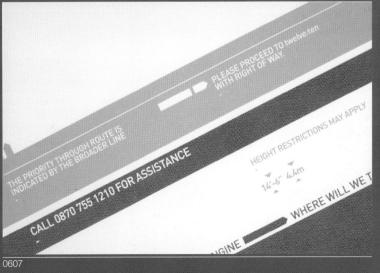

0607

0608   0609

NB:Studio
UK

Duffy Singapore
Singapore

0610

Pangaro Beer
USA

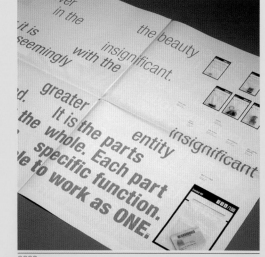

0608

0609

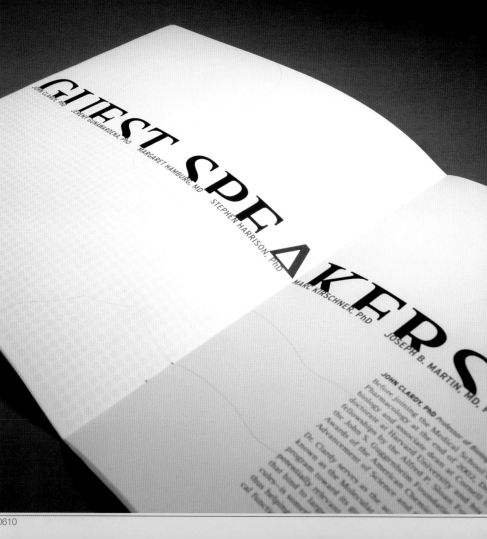

0610

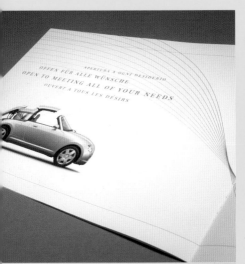

611

0613

0615

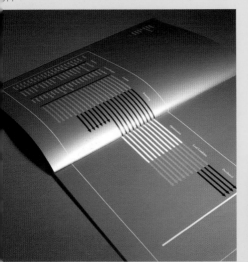

612

0614

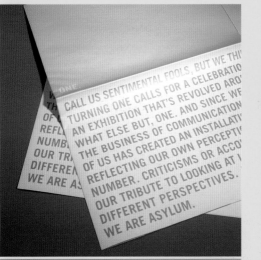

0616

BY MALENE BIRGER
BY WHIITE
KUDIBAL

TIGER OF SWEDEN
LUNDGREN & WINDINGE
PINK SODA
SASHA FEDER

PORTE À GAUCHE

JANE KÖNIG
JULIE SANDLAU

SEQOUIA
SALT

18

0619
Harcus Design
Australia

↘↘

0620
Muggie Ramadani Design Studio
Denmark

↘

0621
Guru Design
Denmark

↘↘

186/187

1000
Brochures

0618

0620

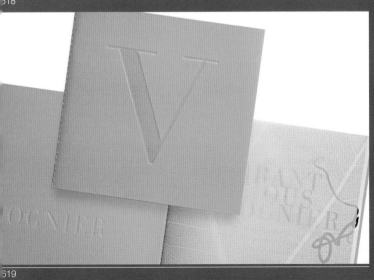

619

0621

0622
Cahan & Associates
USA
↘

0623
Cahan & Associates
USA
↘↘

0624
Cahan & Associates
USA
↘

0625
Muggie Ramadani Design Studio
Denmark
↘↘

0622

0624

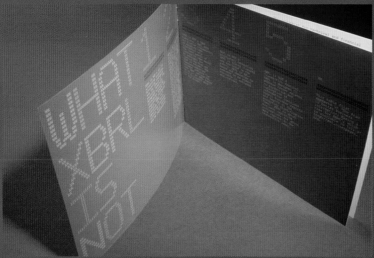

0623

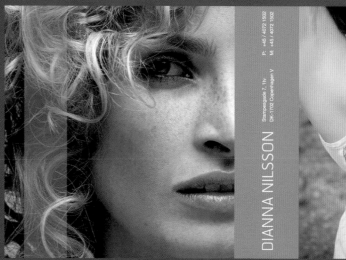

0625

26
4 Design, LLC
A

0627
Design Depot Creative Bureau
Russia

0628
Design Depot Creative Bureau
Russia

0629
Design Depot Creative Bureau
Russia

188/189
1,000 Brochures

02 : tina

Tina: I want to thank Simon for suggesting 'Stand By You' as a duet with Hannah, StarGate for doing such a great job on the production. Cathy Dennis and Danny D for writing and producing 'I'll Be There'. Gayle for being them for me and the band. My band friends Zoe, Louise and Andrew. My boyfriend Jason, Polydor and 19 Management for believing in us. Most of all I want to thank my parents and not forgetting the fans — your support has been amazing!

0626

Once
we
accept our
limits, go
we beyond
them

accept our limits, go we beyond them
Albert Einstein

0628

Don't
be afraid
to give up
the good
to go for
the
great

John D. Rockefeller

The ■
price
of is
greatness responsibility
Sir Winston Churchill

0630
Hartford Design, Inc.
USA

0631
Segura Inc.
USA

0632
Hartford Design, Inc.
USA

0630

0631

0632

33

0635

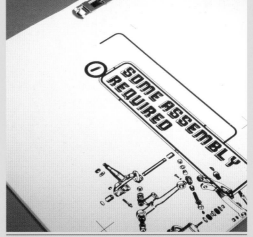

0637

34

0636

0638

0639

0640

0641

0642

0643

0644

45 0646
IsonHarvey/Loewy WilsonHarvey/Loewy
UK

0647 0648
AdamsMorioka, Inc. Wonksite
USA Colombia

0649 0650
Underware Wonksite
The Netherlands Colombia

192/193
1000
Brochures

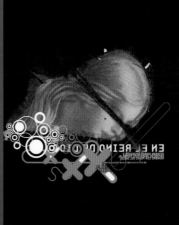

45

0647

0649

WHO SHOULD ATTEND:

The Information for Profit Summit 2004 has been exclusively developed for Chief Financial Officers and Chief Information Officers operating in leading blue chip organisations across Europe. Use this seminar to align your IT and Finance functions and improve the long term performance of your organisation. Places are limited and are only available to invited delegates. Register immediately using the enclosed faxback form or contact our registration hotline on 020 7420 7700 to ensure your place at the summit.

WHY ATTEND:

THE INFORMATION FOR PROFIT SUMMIT 2004 OFFERS A STRATEGIC HIGH VALUE AGENDA TO HELP YOU REALISE THE VALUE OF YOUR INFORMATION ENTERPRISE-WIDE. OUR PANEL OF SPEAKERS HAS BEEN SELECTED TO OFFER INSIGHT AND PRACTICAL ADVICE TO HELP YOU CONVERT INFORMATION INTO HARD CURRENCY COMBINING STRATEGIC CONSULTING CASE EXPERIENCE AND TECHNICAL ADVICE. THIS SEMINAR WILL MAKE YOU RE-EVALUATE YOUR ORGANISATIONS STRATEGIC DECISION-MAKING PROCESSES FOR IMPROVED REVENUE GROWTH AND A GREATER RETURN ON YOUR ASSETS.

FORMATION FOR PROFIT 2004:
INFORMATION FOR PROFIT SUMMIT 2004 IS AN EXCLUSIVE BREAK BRIEFING FOR EXECUTIVES LOOKING TO ACHIEVE COMPETITIVE TAGE THROUGH IMPROVED INFORMATION MANAGEMENT AND ION-MAKING. SCHEDULED FOR THE 25TH FEBRUARY, THIS EVENT EEN SPECIALLY FORMULATED BY LEADING SOLUTION PROVIDER

46

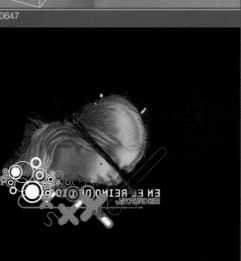

0648

0650

0651
Voice
Australia
↘

0652
Voice
Australia
↘

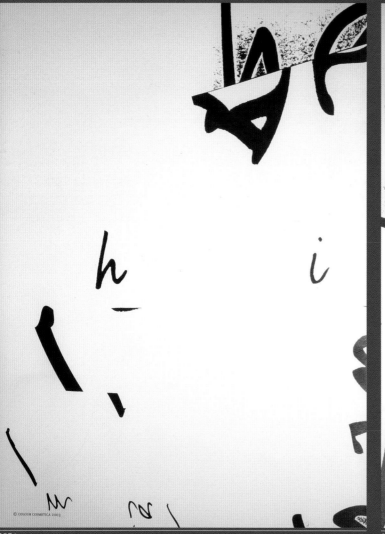

SECTION B

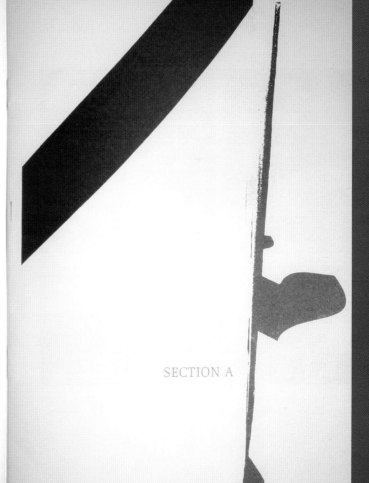

print media / session styling

pr   m ia/

print media / session styling

prin t m edia/
sess ion styl i ng

SECTION A

0654
Cahan & Associates
USA
⌄ ⌄

0655
Cahan & Associates
USA
⌄⌄ ⌄

0656
SalterBaxter
UK
⌄ ⌄

0657
Motive Design Research
USA
⌄⌄ ⌄⌄

0645

0655

0656

0657

INNOVATIVE BUSINESS MODELS HAVE BEEN

THE NORM WITH HERMAN MILLER FROM OUR MOV

INTO "MODERN" FURNITURE IN THE 1930S,

TO OUR TRANSFORMATION OF THE OFFICE

FURNITURE INDUSTRY IN THE 1970S, TO THE "SI

QUICK, AND AFFORDABLE" SUCCESSES OF THE

1990S. HERMAN MILLER RED IS NOW INTRODU

US TO A FRESH SET OF CUSTOMERS WITH NE

CHANNELS TO MARKET, HIP NEW PRODUCT

AN ATTITUDE TO MATCH.

0659

0661

0660

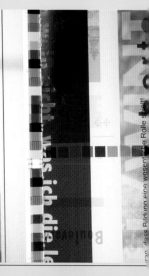

0662

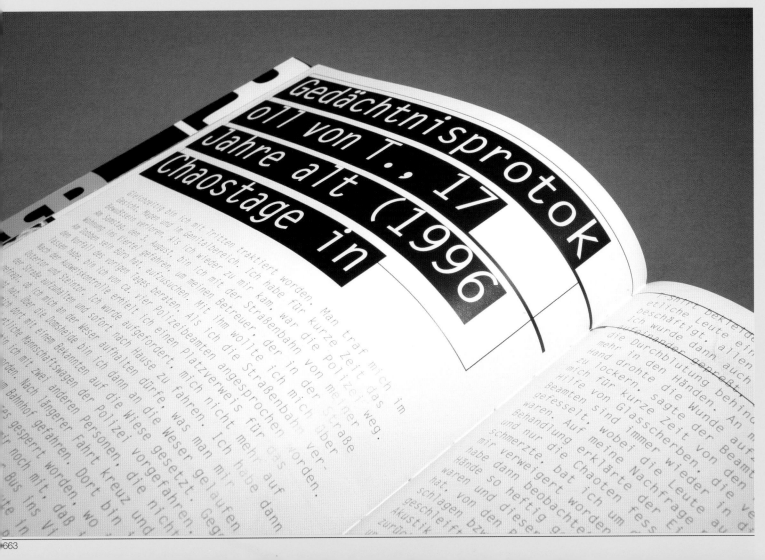

0664

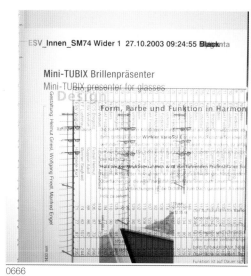

0666

0668

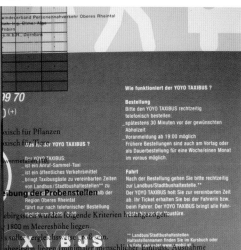

0665

0667

0669

70
Works Design
mmunication
ada

0671
Envision+
Germany

0672
Starshot
Germany

0673
Motive Design Research
USA

200/201

1000
Brochures

70

0672

671

0673

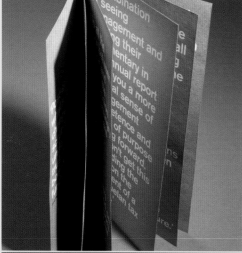

0674

0675

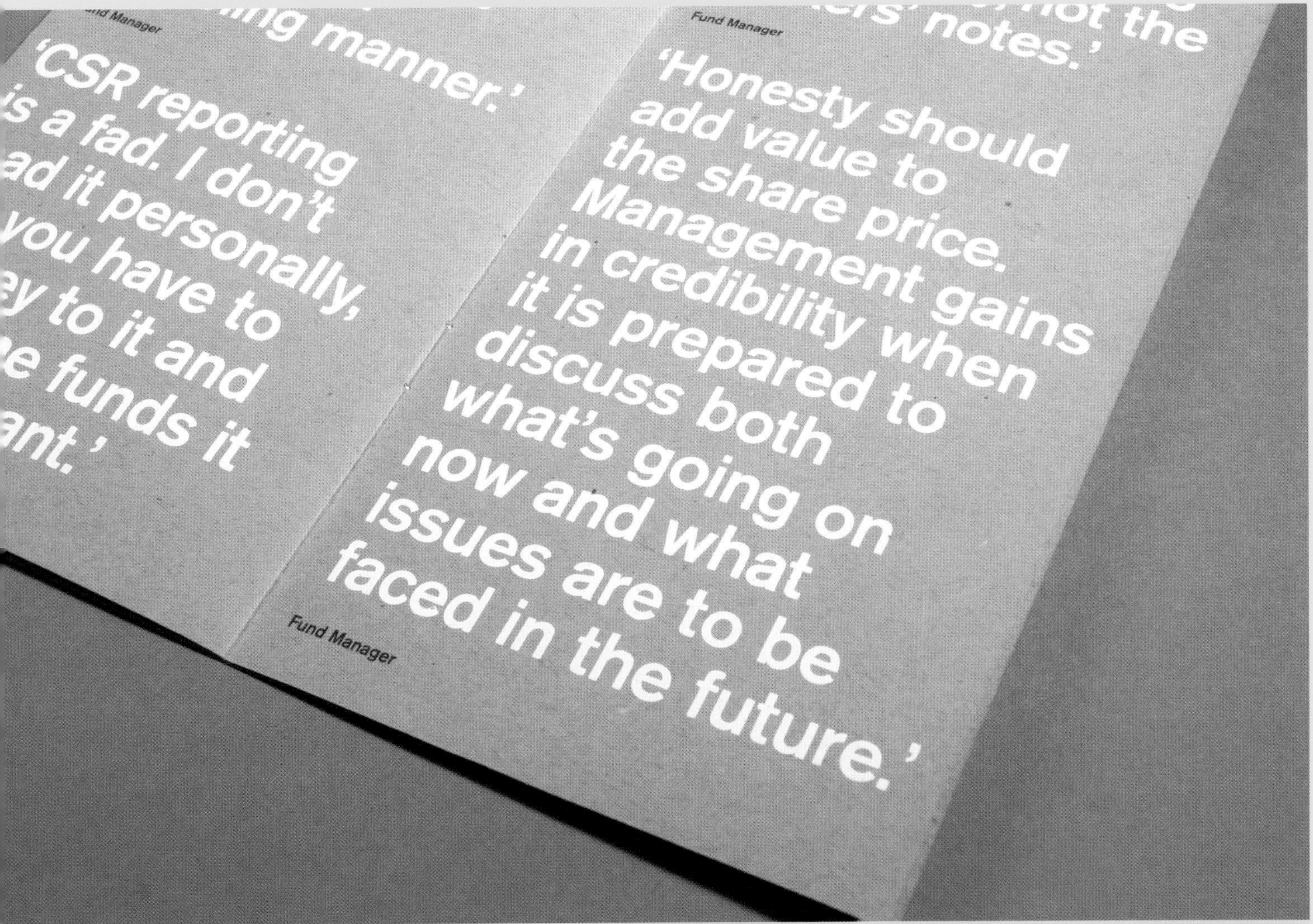

'CSR reporting is a fad. I don't [...] it personally, [...] you have to [...] to it and [...] funds it [...]'

Fund Manager

'Honesty should add value to the share price. Management gains in credibility when it is prepared to discuss both what's going on now and what issues are to be faced in the future.'

Fund Manager

P C M   publicité club de mon-

tréal

#44

CONCOURS DU PCM

79 | 0680 | 0681 | 0682 | 0683 | 0684 | 204/205

cle K Studio | **KROG** Slovenia | **Ligalux GmbH** Germany | **Ligalux GmbH** Germany | **Ligalux GmbH** Germany | **Ligalux GmbH** Germany | 1000 Brochures

79

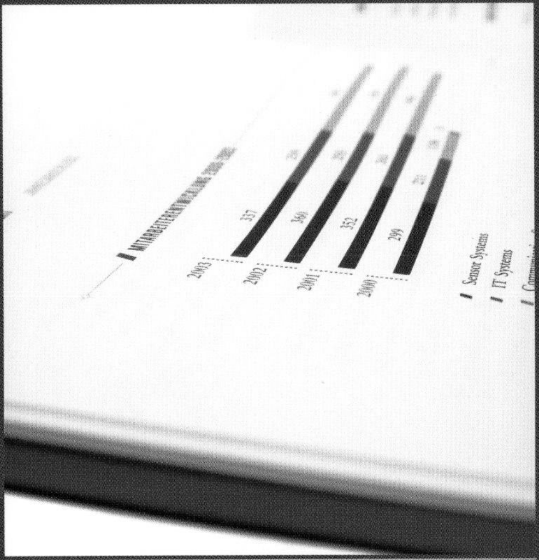

0681

0683

80

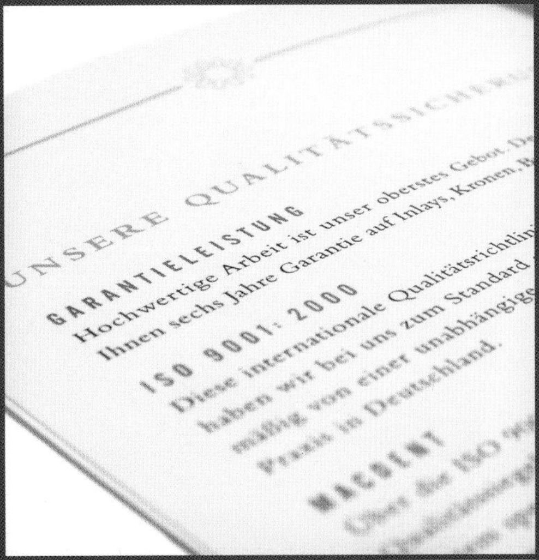

0682

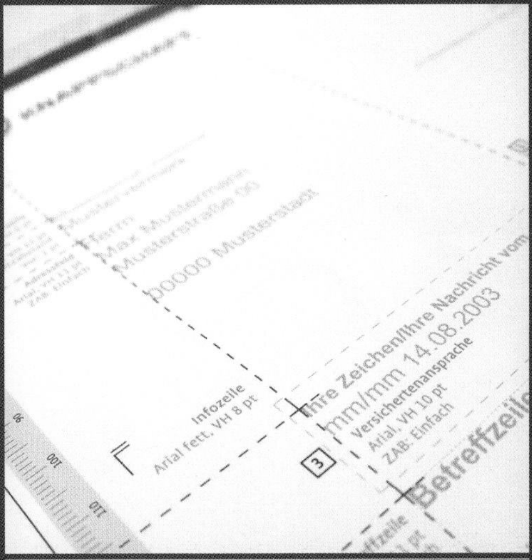

0684

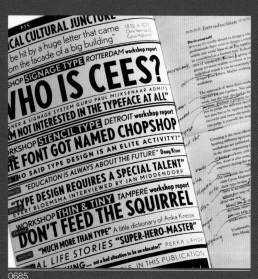

0685

0687

0689

0686

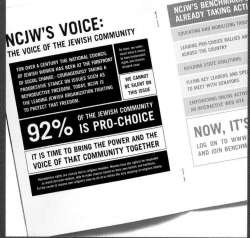

0688

0690

91
d Partners

0692
The Family Design International
UK
↘ ↘

0693
Guru Design
Denmark
↘

0694
The Family Design International
UK
↘ ↘

206/207
1000 Brochures

FIND YOUR VOICE. IT'S | TIME TO SPEAK OUT
AND FIGHT BACK. ON | JANUARY 22, 1973
THE SUPREME COURT | AFFIRMED WOMEN'S
CONSTITUTIONAL RIGHT | TO ABORTION
IN ITS LANDMARK *ROE* | *V. WADE* RULING.
TODAY THIS RIGHT IS | UNDER ATTACK IN
COURTROOMS ACROSS | THE COUNTRY. YOU
CAN DO SOMETHING | ABOUT IT. TAKE
ACTION TODAY, BEFORE | IT'S TOO LATE.

0695
Eggers & Diaper
Germany

↘

0696
Dulude
Canada

↘

_self_promo

inière

HOTOGRAPHE

ariane's cup
2002
19-24·09·02

21·9	heiligenhafen-travemünde
22·9	travemünde-grömitz
23·9	grömitz-heiligenhafen
	www.arianecup2002.com

0698
Ligalux GmbH
Germany
↘

0699
Ligalux GmbH
Germany
↘↘

0700
Ligalux GmbH
Germany
↘

0701
Ligalux GmbH
Germany
↘↘

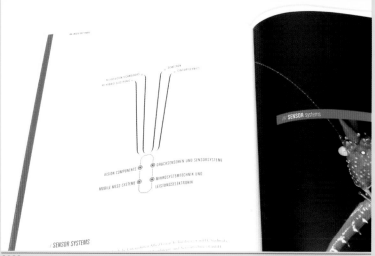

/ SENSOR SYSTEMS

0698

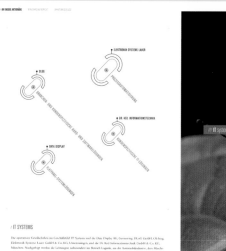

/ IT SYSTEMS

Die operative Gesellschaften im Geschäftsfeld IT Systems sind die Data Display AG, Germering, DLoG GmbH, Olching, Elektronik-Systeme Lauer GmbH & Co. KG, Unterensingen, und die Dr. Keil Informationstechnik GmbH & Co. KG, München. Nachgefragt werden die Leistungen insbesondere im Bereich Logistik, im Automobilsektor, dem Maschinenbau, der Elektroindustrie sowie der Luft- und Raumfahrt.

0700

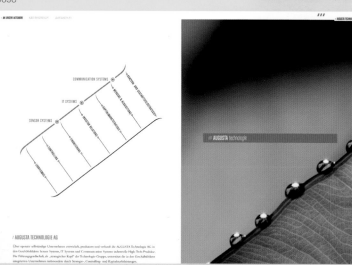

/ AUGUSTA TECHNOLOGIE AG

Über unsere abhängige Unternehmen entwickelt, produziert und verkauft die AUGUSTA Technologie AG in den Geschäftsfeldern Sensor Systems, IT Systems und Communication Systems industrielle High-Tech-Produkte. Die Führungsgesellschaft, als "strategischer Kopf" der Technologie-Gruppe, unterstützt die in den Geschäftsfeldern integrierten Unternehmen insbesondere durch Strategie-, Controlling- und Kapitalaufteilungen.

0699

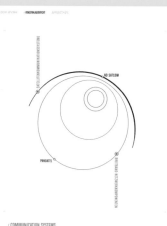

/ COMMUNICATION SYSTEMS

Während die mobilen und stationären Satellitenkommunikationssysteme von der NEO SatCom AG, hammermand, entwickelt werden, stammen die Multiplexer und Netzwerkkomponenten die Kapfer-, die auch für Gläubiger von der Pandatel AG, Hamburg. Kunden des Geschäftsfelds Communication Systems sind insbesondere multinational agierende Konzerne, Telekommunikationsanstalter und Netzbetreiber sowie TV-Anstalten und staatliche Organisationen.

0701

°02
galux GmbH
rmany

0703
Ligalux GmbH
Germany

0704
Untitled
UK

210/211
1000
Brochures

CONSULTING

ı o6.07 The Code of Communications

CONSULTING

0702

0703

0704

NO ONE WAY

NO ONE DE

PLEASE OBEY THE_
COUNTRY CODE_

TO READ MAGENTA
OVERPRINT TEXT, FLIP
THIS PAGE 180°

06

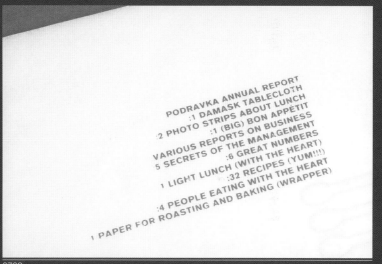

0708

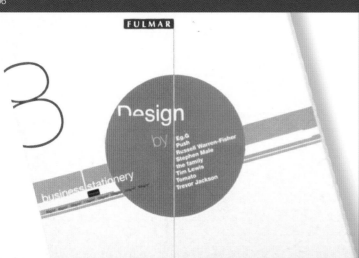

07   0709

0710
Cahan & Associates
USA

0711
Capsule
USA

0712
Mires
USA

0713
Cahan & Associates
USA

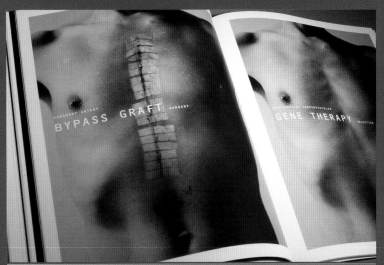

0710

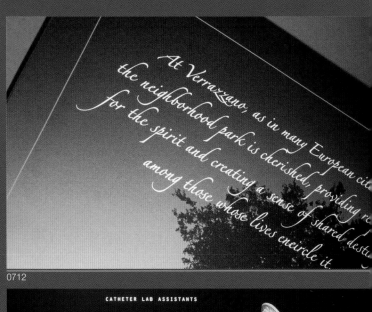

0712

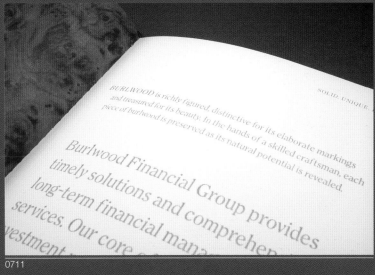

0711

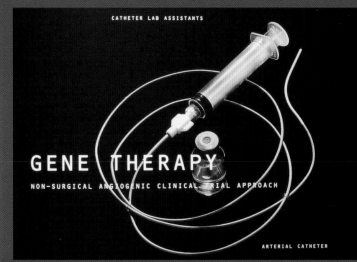

0713

14   0715
fy Singapore   **Starshot**
apore   Germany

0716   0717
Starshot   iridium, a design agency
Germany   Canada

214/215
1000 Brochures

14

64

ZZ.7.Z003

IN LOVE?

LARA top: hot MATADOR, bag SIGG
LARA with SAECO CANNONDALE rider Jörg Ludewig
travelling in the SAECO team bus: blouse MARLBORO
CLASSICS

0716

18¹⁹

10.7.2003

NEVERS

5th stage Dinner with the whole Team Saeco. Next to Lara, clockwise: Gerrit Glomser, Paolo Fornaciari, Fabio Sacchi, Jörg
from left VERENA: shorts PUMA, pullover QUIKSILVER, sandals BETULA ; LARA: tank top PUMA

15

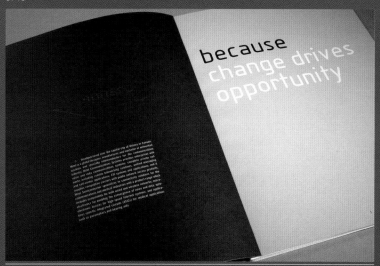

because
change drives
opportunity

0717

0718
**KearneyRocholl Corporate
Communications AG**
Germany

0719
**KearneyRocholl Corporate
Communications AG**
Germany

0720
**KearneyRocholl Corporate
Communications AG**
Germany

0718

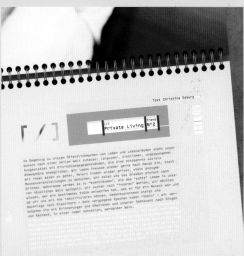

0719

0720

| 1 | 0722 | 0723 | 0724 | 0725 | 0726 | 216/217 |

...mese Design | **Usine de Boutons** | **Sommese Design** | **KearneyRocholl Corporate | **Viva Dolan Communications** | **KearneyRocholl Corporate** | 1000

Italy | USA | Communications AG** | **& Design Inc.** | Communications AG** | Brochures

Germany | Canada | Germany

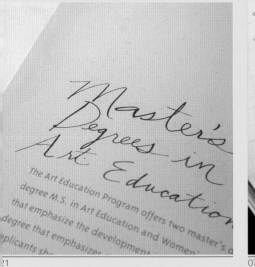

...21

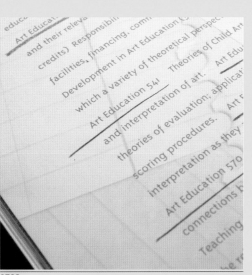

0723

0725

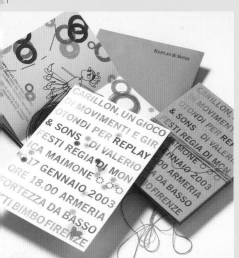

...22

0724

0726

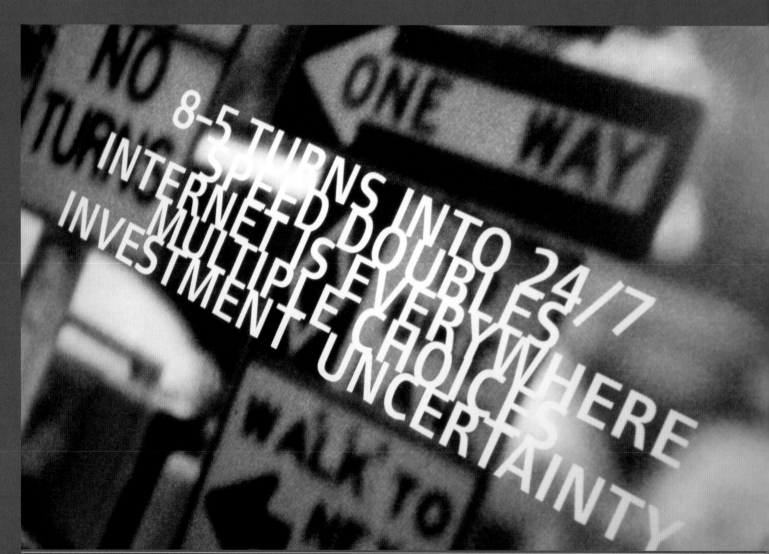

28

0730

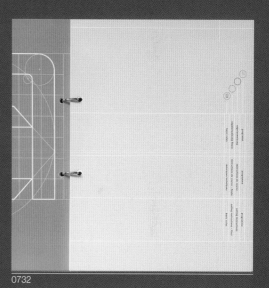

0732

29

0731

0733

0734
Strichpunkt
Germany

0735
Strichpunkt
Germany

0736
AdamsMorioka, Inc.
USA

0734

0735

CAITLIN'S WAY

Tonight 9:00/8:00c

letterspacing is not perfect

Secondary typography
simple **block serif fonts**
all upper and lowercase
direct, raw, energetic
industrial, straightforward
NOT decorative, fussy or digital

Font choices
City
Clarendon
Courier
Memphis
Officina Serif
Rockwell

Primary typography
simple **sans serif fonts**
all uppercase
direct, raw, energetic
industrial, straightforward
NOT decorative, fussy or digital

Font choices
Airport
Bell Gothic
Folio
Franklin Gothic
Monotype Grotesque
News Gothic
Standard
Trade Gothic
Venus

Nickelodeon
Typography

0736

0737
KearneyRocholl Corporate
Communications AG
Germany

0738
And Partners
USA

0739
design hoch drei GmbH & Co. KG
Germany

0740
Strichpunkt
Germany

220/221

1000
Brochures

0737

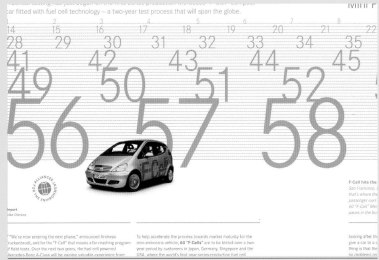

0739

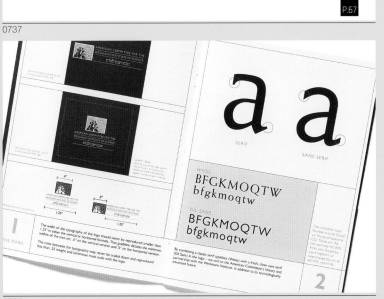

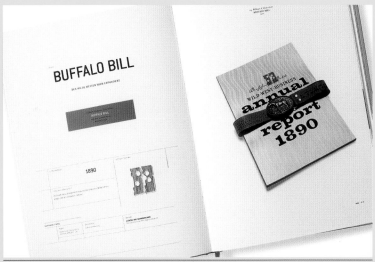

{ CONTENTS }
*

04
A NOTE FROM THE CHANCELLOR

05
FORWARD
Dr. Annette Stott
Director, School of Art and Art History

07
MULTICULTURALISM: **THE SEARCH FOR** ETHNIC, SEXUAL AND RACIAL **IDENTITY IN A POSTMODERN WORLD**
Kent Logan

11
ROBERT COLESCOTT & **GLENN LIGON** ✳ CONFRONTING **CARICATURE** & **STEREOTYPE**
Dr. Shannen Hill
Director, Victoria H. Myhren Gallery

20
PLATES

30
ARTIST BIOGRAPHIES: ROBERT COLESCOTT, GLENN LIGON

32
WORKS IN THE EXHIBITION

*

ROBERT **COLESCOTT** &
& GLENN **LIGON**

FROM THE **LOGAN** COLLECTION

UNIVERSITY OF DENVER
VICTORIA H. MYHREN GALLERY

JANUARY 9–FEBRUARY 27

#1010
REVERSIBLE

#3010
CHAPEAU - HAT

0744
Starshot
Germany
↘

0745
Starshot
Germany
↘

0746
Twelve: Ten
UK
↘↘

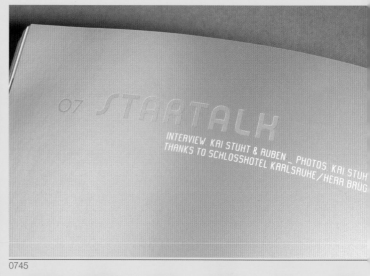

0745

ttG03 ●
Scale 1:500

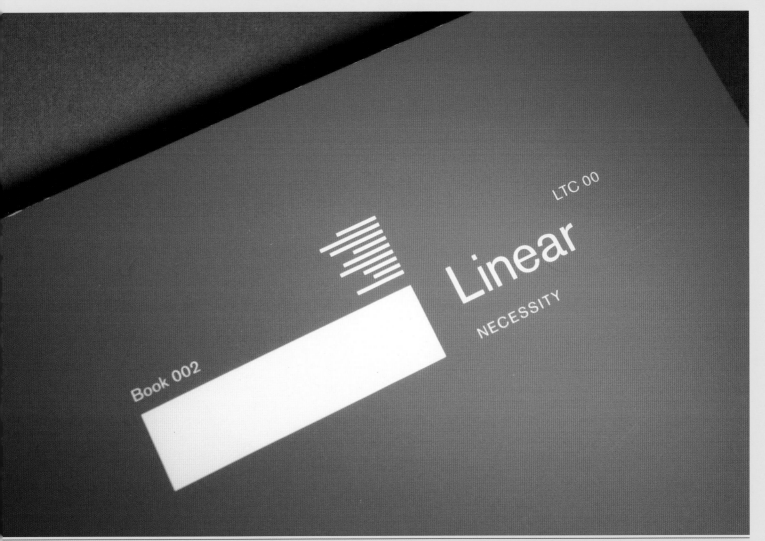

>

Chapter 5.
Posters + banners.

>

—

>

Posters

Banners

>

>

/// O Centro Cultural Justiça Federal apresenta

Balet de Pincela /// Michele Petruccelli

60 centavos o grama /// Yomar Augusto

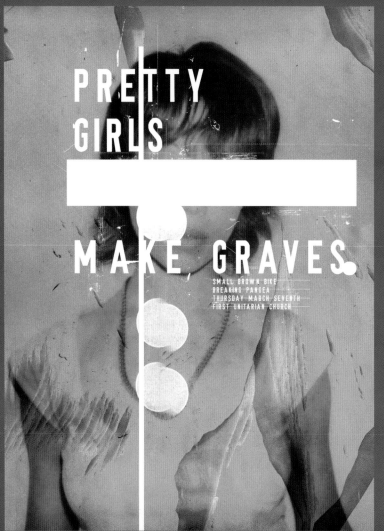

FLY FISHE
DON'T KN
DON'T CA
STRAIGH
THE MIDI
BUTTFUD
NOWHER
IN MY PAN
FEELING I
PHILLIST
EYES EMP
EVERY DO
A GUILLO
READIN'T
PHONE B
WONDER

BUCK
65 TALKIN'
HONKY
BLUES

0751
Beautiful
UK

0752
Beautiful
UK

0753
Beautiful
UK

0754
Beautiful
UK

0751

0753

0752

0754

0756
Beautiful
UK
↘

0757
Beautiful
UK
↘↘

230/231
1000
Posters +
banners

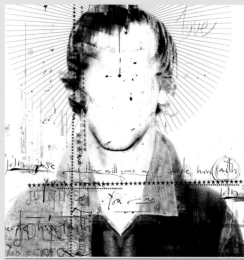

0756

0758

0760

0762

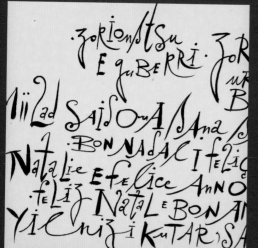

0759

0761

0763

'64
Ogura Inc.
A

0765
Design Center Ltd.
Slovenia

0766
Polite Design
Incorporated
USA

0767
Cheng Design
USA

0768
NB:Studio
UK

0769
Cheng Design
USA

232/233
1000
Posters +
banners

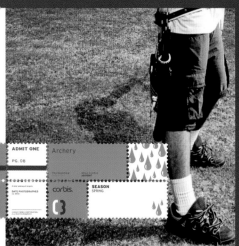

'64

0766

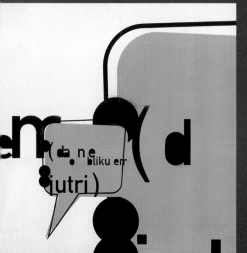

'65

0767

0769

0768

71 | 0772 | 0773 | 0774 | 234/235
lude | **IRBE Design** | **Joe Miller's Company** | **Dulude** | 1000 posters + banners
nada | USA | USA | Canada

⤓⤓ | ⤓⤓

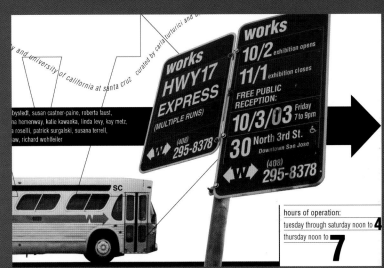

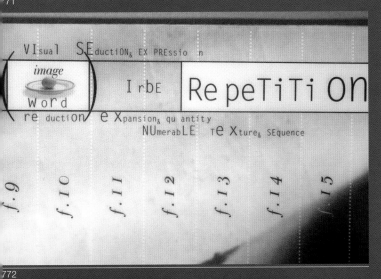

0775
A3 Design
USA

0776
Harrimansteel
UK

0777
Wolken Communica
USA

0778
IAAH/iamalwayshungry
USA

0775

0777

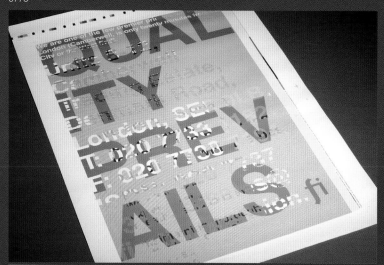

0776

0778

79

0780
Cheng Design
USA
⌄⌄

0781
A3 Design
USA
⌄⌄

0782
Harrimansteel
UK
⌄⌄

236/237
1000
Posters +
banners

rrimansteel

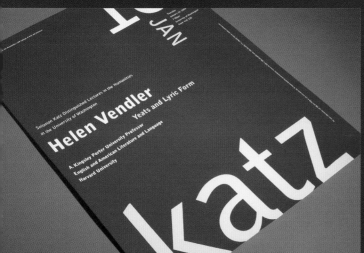

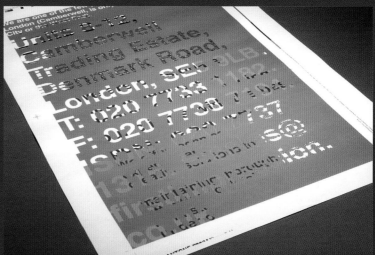

0783
Origin
UK

0784
Origin
UK

0785
Piscatello Design Centre
USA

0783

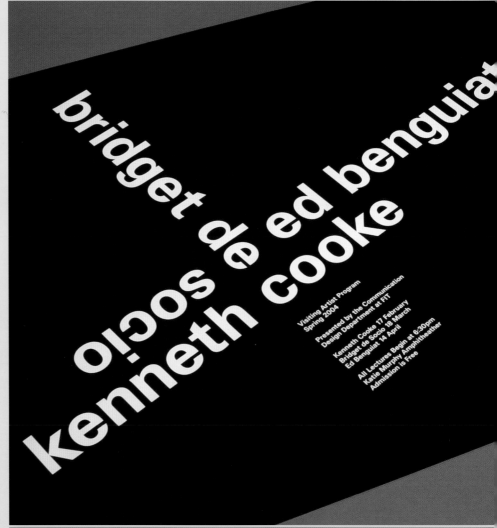

0784

0785

0786

0788

0790

0787

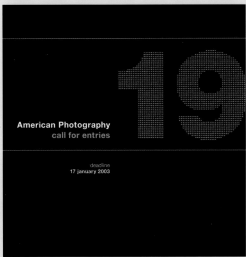

American Photography
call for entries

deadline
17 january 2003

0789

0791

93   0794
Niklaus Troxler Design   Gervais
zerland   The Netherlands

0795   0796
Niklaus Troxler Design   Niklaus Troxler Design
Switzerland   Switzerland

0797   0798
Niklaus Troxler Design   Gervais
Switzerland   The Netherlands

240/241

1000
Posters +
banners

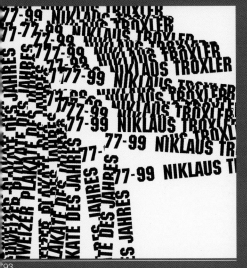

'93

0795

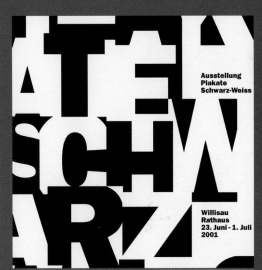

0797

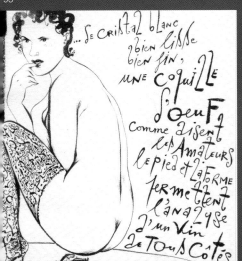

94

0796

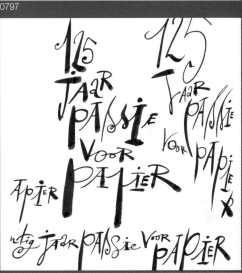

0798

0799
Sagmeister Inc.
USA
↘

0800
NB:Studio
UK
↘ ↘

0801
the commissary
USA
↘

0802
Segura Inc.
USA
↘ ↘

0799

0801

0800

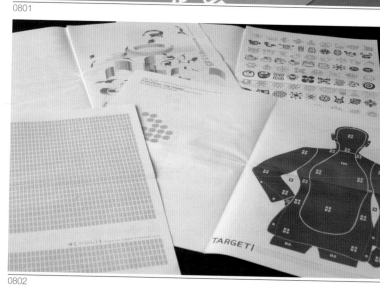

0802

03 | 0804 | 0805 | 0806 | 0807 | 0808 | 242/243

Design | Mehdi Saeedi | Carter Wong Tomlin | Segura Inc. | Carter Wong Tomlin | Sagmeister Inc. | 1000 posters + banners
Iran | UK | USA | UK | USA
xico

603

0805

0807

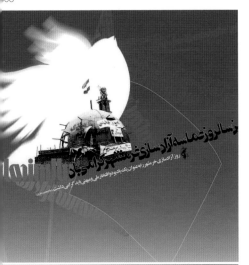

304

0806

0808

0809
vo6
Brazil

0810
vo6
Brazil

0811
Mehdi Saeedi
Iran

0812
vo6
Brazil

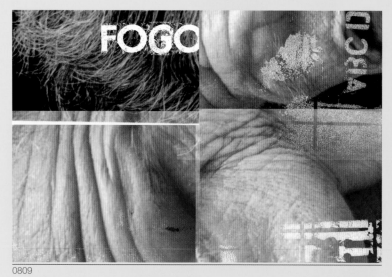

0809

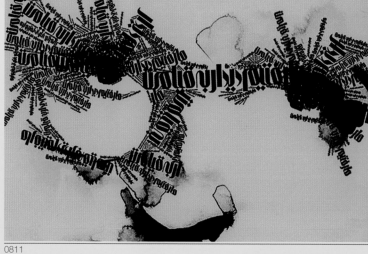

0811

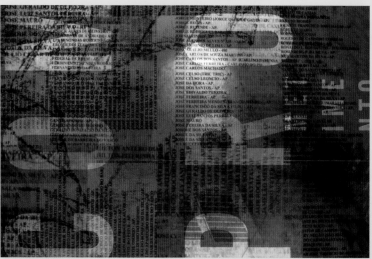

0810

0812

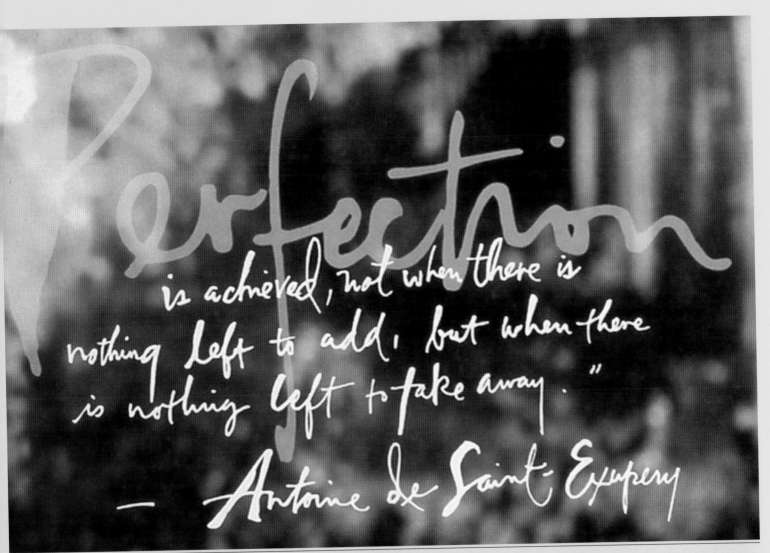

Perfection is achieved, not when there is nothing left to add, but when there is nothing left to take away."

— Antoine de Saint-Exupéry

0812

0814
Lippa Pearce Design,
London
UK

0815
Insight Design Communications
USA

0816
Wonksite
Colombia

0817
Segura Inc.
USA

0818
Enspace, Inc.
USA

0819
the commissary
USA

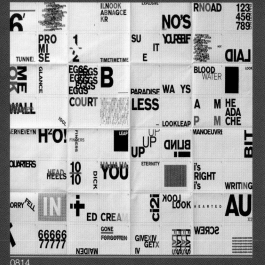

0814

0816

0818

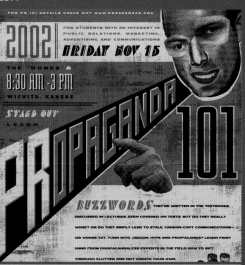

0815

0817

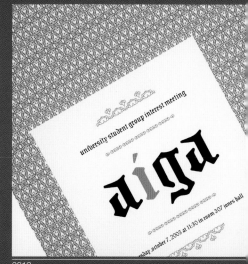

0819

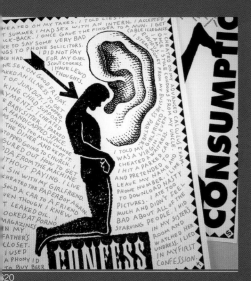

320

0822

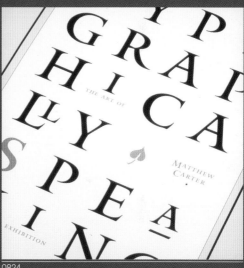

0824

321

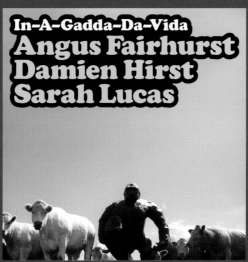

0823

0825

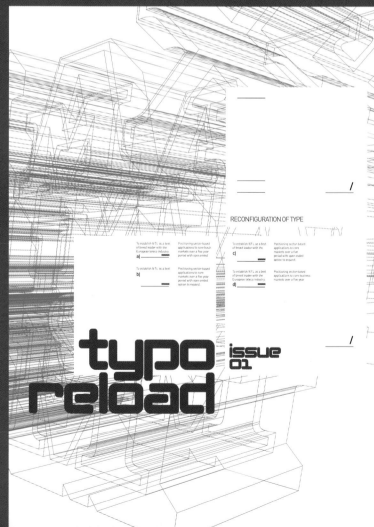

RECONFIGURATION OF TYPE

a) To establish NTL as a best of breed leader with the European telecoms industry.

Positioning sector-based applications to core business markets over a five year period with open ended

b) To establish NTL as a best

Positioning sector-based applications to core markets over a five year period with open ended option to expand.

c) To establish NTL as a best of breed leader with the

Positioning sector-based applications to core markets over a five period with open ended option to expand.

d) To establish NTL as a best of breed leader with the European telecoms industry.

Positioning sector-based applications to core business markets over a five year

typo reload issue 01

0829
the commissary
USA

0830
the commissary
USA

0831
the commissary
USA

0832
ALR Design
USA

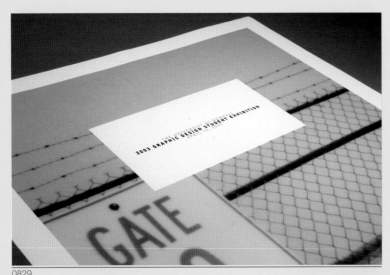

0829

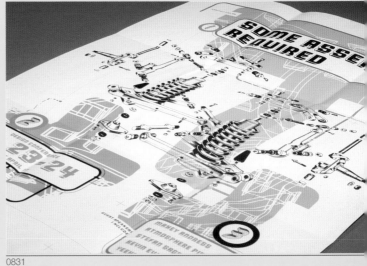

0831

0830

0832

0834
the commissary
USA

0835
the commissary
USA

250/251
1000
posters +
banners

0833

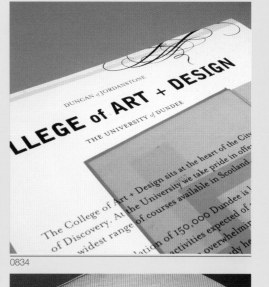

0834

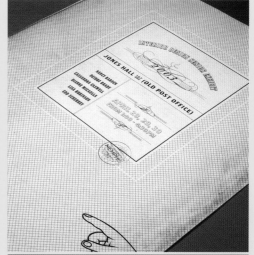

0835

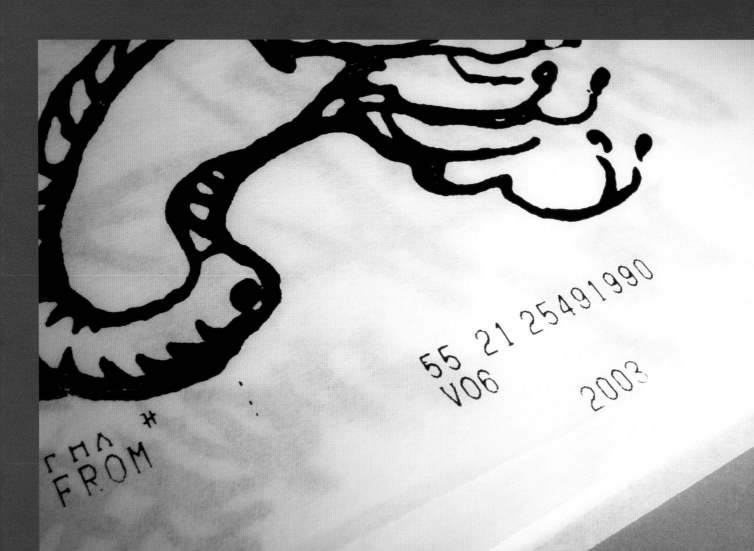

37
KearneyRocholl Corporate
Communications AG
Germany

0838
Joe Miller's Company
USA
↘↘

0839
Joe Miller's Company
USA
↘

0840
KearneyRocholl Corporate
Communications AG
Germany
↘↘

252/253
1000
Posters +
banners

0837

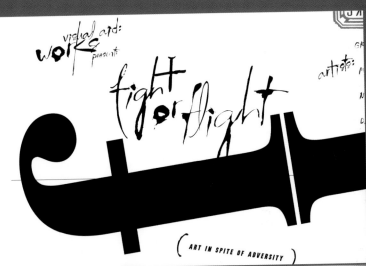

0839

0840

0841
Dulude
Canada

0842
Iron Design
USA

0843
Capsule
USA

0844
Capsule
USA

0841

0843

0842

0844

345
ush Design

0846
Wonksite
Colombia

0847
Sagmeister Inc.
USA

0848
Wonksite
Colombia

254/255
1000
Posters +
banners

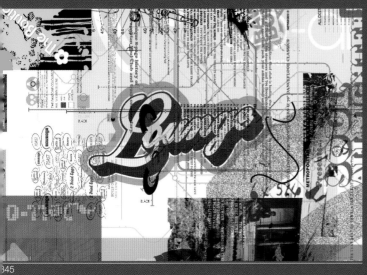

0345

0847

346

0848

0849

0850

0851

0852

0854

0856

0853

0855

0857

0859

0860
Modern Dog
USA

0861
KearneyRocholl Corporate
Communications AG
Germany

0862
KearneyRocholl Corporate
Communications AG
Germany

0863
KearneyRocholl Corporate
Communications AG
Germany

0864
Modern Dog
USA

258/259
1000
Posters +
banners

0859

0861

0863

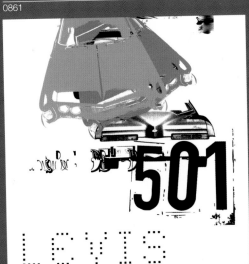

0862

0864

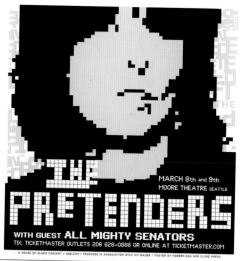

0865

0867

0869

0866

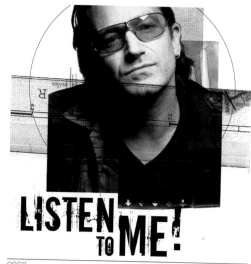

0868

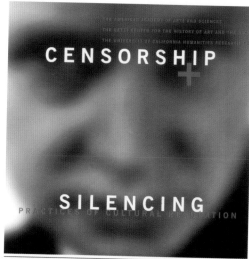

0870

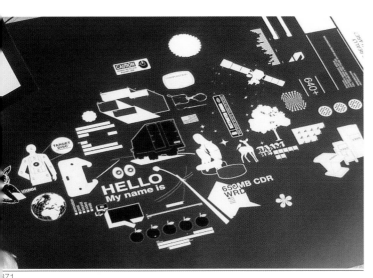

371

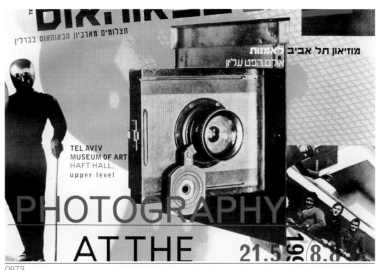

0873

372

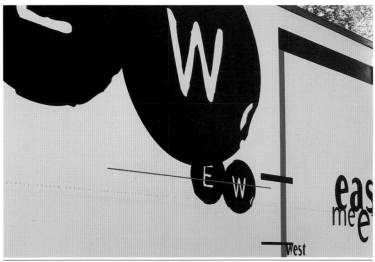

0874

0875

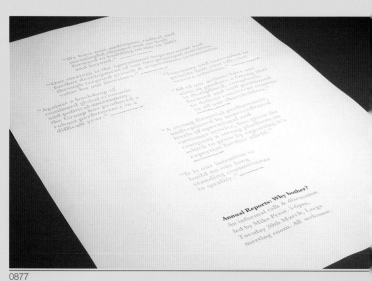

0877

0876

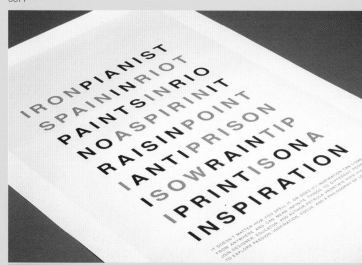

0878

0880
Joe Miller's Company
USA
↘

0881
344 Design, LLC
USA
↘↘

0882
Juan Torneros
Colombia
↘

0883
Segura Inc.
USA
↘↘

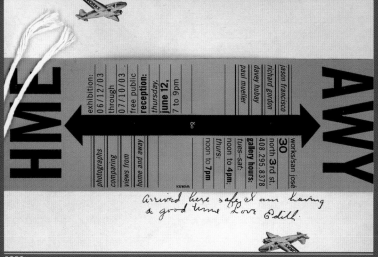

0880

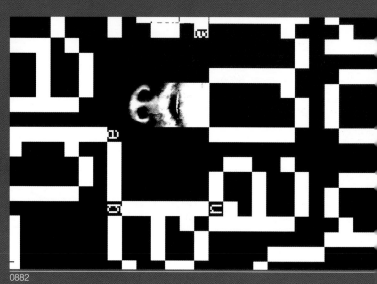

0882

0881

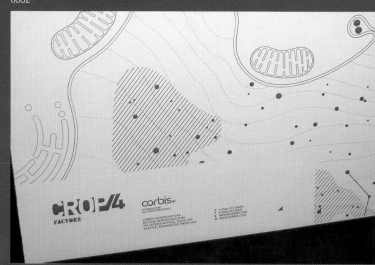

0883

84　　　　　　0885
gura Inc.　　　KearneyRocholl Corporate Communications AG
　　　　　　　Germany

↘↘

0886　　　　　0887
Segura Inc.　　KearneyRocholl Corporate Communications AG
USA　　　　　Germany
↘　　　　　　↘↘

264/265

:1000+
posters +
banners

84

0886

85

0887

Chapter 6.
3D + outdoor + digital.

0888–1000

Packaging

1000

Websites

Signage

Film

Outdoor

Large format

Television

3D

0891
unit9
UK

0892
Zip Design Ltd
UK

0893
Atelier Works
UK

0894
344 Design, LLC
USA

.1 GUNS FOR GUITARS

JUST NEED A CROWD, A GANG, A REASON TO SMILE..." JOURNAL

Cobain felt utterly cast adrift as his parents built new families with new partners. Music was an escape and a salvation, and, almost immediately, he began to forge songs from nuggets of personal experience. Latterly, Nirvana's Sliver (first widely available on the compilation Incesticide) captured the dislocation of a trip to his grandparents' house, while Something in the Way mythologises a period of emotional and physical teenage limbo.

< 1 2 3 4 >

0891

SLADE GARDENS
ADVENTURE PLAYGROUND

CHATTING JOKING MEETING BUILDING SMILING LAUGHING CHILLING MUNCHING MAKING SWINGING RELAXING DRAWING LEARNING READING DESIGNING EXERCISING PLAYING COOKING RUNNING JUMPING THINKING SLIDING DIGGING CLIMBING DISCOVERING PAINTING CRAFTING

0893

DIO ONLY
RASSIC 22 CDP
WWW.LOFIDELITYALLSTARS.CO.UK

WHAT YOU WANT
DEEP ELLUM... HOLD ON [FEAT. JAMIE LIDEL
LO FI'S IN IBIZA
SOMEBODY NEEDS YOU [FEAT. GREG DULL
DON'T BE AFRAID OF LOVE
FEEL WHAT I FEEL [FEAT. BOOTSY
ON THE PIER
JUST ENOUGH

0892

DEPARTMENT OF
Revolutionary, worldwide unique
New TECHNOLOG

It's so simple.

Bang, You're Alive!

0894

895

0896
elton Communication

Lippa Pearce Design, London
UK

0897
Hoyne Design
Australia

0898
Machine
The Netherlands

270/271

:1000
:3D +
:outdoor +
digital

SYPHILIS! SEX PESTS USED TO RUT LIKE DOGS N HEAT AND NOT WORRY ABOUT THIS BLEEDIN' BUG. BUT NOW SYPHILIS IS REARING ITS UGLY HEAD MONG US DIRTY BASTARDS. AND IT AIN'T GOING A

0895

DYSFUNCTIONAL

K

TO REMOVE THE BIAS FROM THE UNIVERSE, PRESS DOWN
ON THE BLAME RELEASE BUTTON AND TURN THE CENTRE
OF GRAVITY CLOCKWISE. *The bias will slip off easily.*

KEEP THIS BOOKLET HANDY FOR
REFERENCE UNTIL YOU HAVE MASTERED
THE ABILITY TO BE TOO DEMANDING.

0405

WALKING WITH SHOES ON FIRE
CAN'T WAIT TO MEET YOU

SONG LYRIC 04

WALKING WITH SHOES ON FIRE
Walking with shoes on fire
Mercury rising higher
Every step is closer to you
I'm walking with shoes on fire

Has time stopped cold
The moments seem like lifetimes
I crave to hold you
No other thing fills my mind

Chorus
Walking with shoes on fire
Mercury rising higher
Every step is closer to you
I'm walking with shoes on fire

No ache, no cut
Has struck so deeply inside
To see, to touch you

I'm outside, lost in the dark night
An orphan who longs to come home
You draw me, capture and claim me
More than I've ever known

Chorus
Walking with shoes on fire
Mercury rising higher
Every step is closer to you
I'm walking with shoes on fire

Cos it's written in the stars
We'll meet one day
Though I know it's fated
Feels like I have waited
For so long, so long, so long,
so long

Can't wait to meet you
Doesn't matter where you are
I will find you
Cos it's written in the stars
I'm shooting for the sky,
just killing time
(We will find the perfect time)
Til the day I meet you
(Waiting for the day)
Can't wait to meet you

Chorus
Can't wait to meet you, I'm
counting down the days
I sleepwalk beside you, I'm
dreaming of your face
I'm shooting for the sky, just
killing time
'Til the day I meet you
Can't wait to meet you

CAN'T WAIT TO MEET YOU 4:16
Written by Tania Doko & James Roche
(Sony/ATV Publishing)
Peter Kvint (BMG Music Publishing)
Electric guitars – Shannon Trottman and
Jack Jones
Acoustic guitar – Jack Jones

0897

When are you going to sta

Now hear this: whoever tends the fires has got to get tha
if somebody has been burning that fire at both ends
, but does it make
even trying.
commonsensus? The mom behind has finally had her baby!
Welcome to the world, little Horace. – Please remind me-

0896

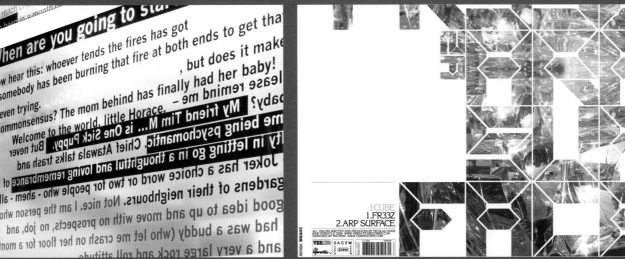

I:CUBE
1.FR33Z
2.ARP SURFACE

VER039

0898

0899
Felton Communication
UK

0900
Why Not Associates
UK

0901
Why Not Associates
UK

0902
Muggie Ramadani Design Studio
Denmark

0899

0900

0901

0902

0903
Why Not Associates & Gordon Young

0904
Why Not Associates
UK

0905
Why Not Associates
UK

272/273
1000
3D +
outdoor +
digital

0903

0904

0905

0906

0908

0910

0907

0909

0911

0912

0914

0913

0915

0917
The Kitchen

0918
Lippa Pearce Design, London
UK

0919
LSD
Spain

0920
Academy of Art University
USA

276/277 : 1000
3D +
outdoor +
digital

0917

0919

0920

0921
unit 9
UK

0922
Hornall Anderson Design Works, Inc.
USA

0923
Why Not Associates
UK

AFTERLI

WHY KURT COBAIN'S SPIRIT LIVES O

BY JAMES KNIGHT OF THE SUNDAY TIMES
AN INTERACTIVE FEATURE IN FOUR CHAPTERS, WITH MORE
THAN 30 MINUTES OF READING, LISTENING AND VIEWING

MOVE ON

0921

0922

✖ Temporada 1950-51:
Fitxatge de Ladislao Kubala

0923

0924
elton Communication

0925
Hornall Anderson Design Works, Inc.
USA

0926
Segura Inc.
USA

0927
unit 9
UK

0928
Segura Inc.
USA

0929
Chermayeff & Geismar Inc.
USA

278/279
1000
3D +
outdoor +
digital

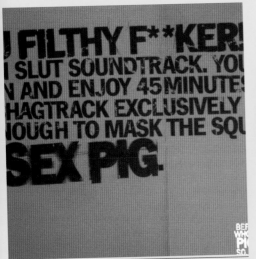

0924

Lesley Spencer's enhanced CD (1), poster (2) and flyer (3), in memory of the September 11th tragedy.

0926

0928

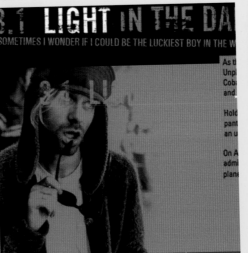

0927

0929

CLARO INTELECTO
PEDESTRIAN 2X12"

PERCENTAGES
RESONATION
AUDRILLARDS SUPPER
RIA
UTUX
SECTION
BACK
2. SECTION
3. YOU NOT ME
SECTION
NOBODY
YOUR TROPHY

0931
egura Inc.
SA

0932
Sweden Graphics
Sweden

0933
Zip Design Ltd
UK

0934
NB: Studio
UK

0935
Sweden Graphics
Sweden

0936
IAAH/iamalwayshungry
USA

280/281
:1000
:3D +
:Outdoor +
:digital

0931

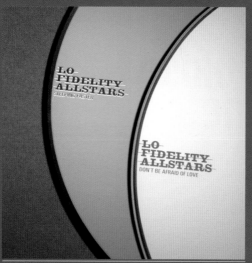

0933

0935

032

0934

0936

0937
Crush Design
UK

0938
WilsonHarvey/Loewy
UK

0939
Crush Design
UK

0940
Plan-B Studio
UK

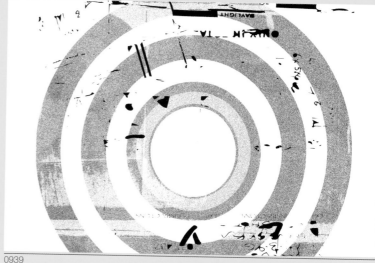

0937

0938

0939

0940

941
WilsonHarvey/Loewy
K

282/283
1000
3D +
outdoor +
digital

0942
Muggie Ramadani
Design Studio
Denmark

0943
Marius Fahrner Design
Germany

0944
Capsule
USA

0945
Crush Design
UK

0946
Ai Records
UK

0947
Motive Design Research
USA

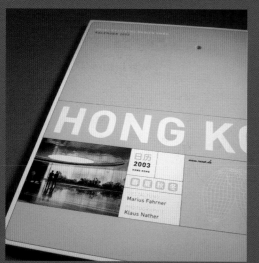
0942

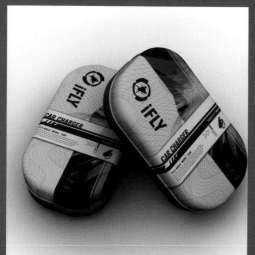
0944

0946

0943

0945

0947

948
Records
UK

0949
Ai Records
UK

0950
Carter Wong Tomlin
UK

0951
Jason Smith
UK

0952
Lippa Pearce Design,
London
UK

0953
Ai Records
UK

284/285
1000
3D +
outdoor +
digital

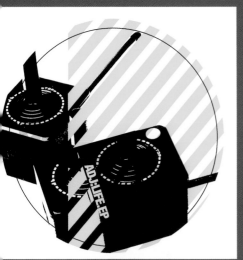

948

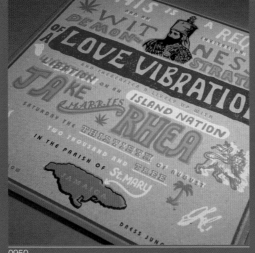

0950

0952

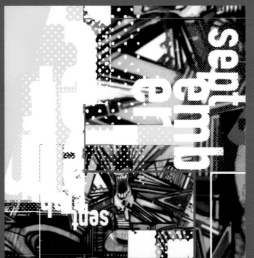

949

0951

0953

FZV:PRECEDENT.

℗ 2004 Ai RECORDS. © 2004 Ai RECORDS. AiLP006. 44KHZ. WRITTEN & PRODUCED BY RICHARD HERBERT. ALL RIGHTS OF THE PRODUCER AND OF THE OWNER OF THE RECORDED WORK RESERVED. UNAUTHORISED COPYING. PUBLIC PERFORMANCE. BROADCASTING. HIRING OR RENTAL OF THIS RECORDING PROHIBITED. DISTRIBUTED BY BAKED GOODS. FOR MORE INFO BUY Ai.RECORDS PRODUCTS VISIT WWW.AIRECORDS.COM / /WWW.ANATHEMATICA.COM

1. METAPHRASTIC.
2. ISO R2.
3. COL MODULUS.
4. AMLGM2.
5. WLTMLT VERSION.
6. COLD.
7. COLDER STILL.
8. CLATR2.
9. SELLS, BORROWS.
10. GOLD TO RUST.
11. F2V.
12. UNTITLED [11.01.01].
13. SHE SAID2.
14. F2V-8BIT.

056

286/287
1000
3D+
outdoor +
digital

0957
Juicy Temples Creative
USA

0958
Juicy Temples Creative
USA

0959
Juicy Temples Creative
USA

0960
Juicy Temples Creative
USA

HEATHER
GOLDEN
A TESTAMENT OF
STRENGTH
+FLEXIBILITY

★ NEW BIZ

STAYS COOL
WHEN THE HEAT'S
TURNED UP
SMOOTH SAILING

CELEBRATE
A GOOD DAY

0957

ANTHONY
DeLAURA
RESIDENT FLASH GURU
ALL AROUND
NICE GUY
DESIGNER

CREATIVE ABILITY
COMPLIMENTS
TECHNICAL
WIZARDRY

★ YES, IT'S DANGEROUS.

0959

WHEN
RANDY
J. HUNT
STROLLS INTO THE STUDIO,
HE BRINGS WITH HIM A COOL CHARM
+YOUTHFUL EXUBERANCE
HIS ENERGY IS CONTAGIOUS
HIS ENTHUSIASM IS INFECTIOUS
AND HE'S A DAMN FINE
DESIGNER
TOO.

★ NOT ANGRY

0958

SIT UP AND
TAKE NOTICE.
KLAUS HEESCH
TWO-FISTED ROGUE
OWNER / ART DIRECTOR
★ HONEST ★
TRUE
PROBLEM
SOLVER

DESIGN
EXPERTISE
CREATIVE WISDOM

MOTORCYCLIST
MUSICIAN
DOG★OWNER

0960

061

IsonHarvey/Loewy

0962
WilsonHarvey/Loewy
UK

0963
WilsonHarvey/Loewy
UK

288/289
1000
3D+
outdoor +
digital

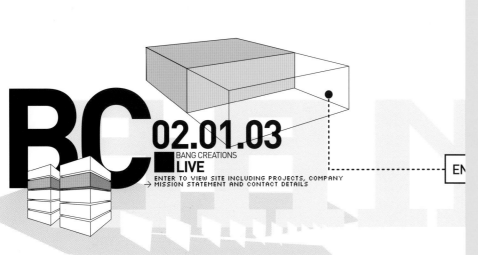

0965
Hoyne Design
Australia

0966
Sweden Graphics
Sweden

0967
Marino A. Gallo
USA

0968
Hoyne Design
Australia

290/291

1000
3D +
outdoor +
digital

0965

0967

0966

0968

0969
Ai Records
UK

0970
Lippa Pearce Design, London
UK

0971
Crush Design
UK

0972
The Family Design International
UK

0969

0970

0971

0972

0973
Non-Format
UK

0974
Plan-B Studio
UK

0975
Ai Records
UK

292/293
1000
3D+
outdoor +
digital

01. Saw Song 02. I Blame You Not 03. Alive 04. Bonding
05. It's Time 06. Lost To Sea 07. June 15 08. Bravely Born(e)
09. Pianni 10. Baby Bloodheart 11. For Me

AC12CD ℗ 2004 Accidental © 2004 Accidental Barcode: 827884001028 Made in EU
www.magicandaccident.com   www.maracarlyle.com

accidental

Mara
Carlyle

The Lovely

DIALeCT

VINYL DIALeCT

0974

CLARO.
INTELECTO.
A1. CHICAGO
A2. SECTION [PART 2]
B1. MONO
B2. SENTI

0975

0976
The Kitchen
UK

0977
Belyea
USA

0978
Segura Inc.
USA

0979
344 Design, LLC
USA

0976

0978

0977

0979

0981
Machine
The Netherlands

0982
Hoyne Design
Australia

294/295
1000
3D +
outdoor +
digital

0981

0983
Wonksite
Colombia

0984
Wonksite
Colombia

0985
KearneyRocholl Corporate Communications AG
Germany

0986
Wonksite
Colombia

0987
Wonksite
Colombia

0988
KearneyRocholl Corporate Communications AG
Germany

0989
Wonksite
Colombia

0990
Wonksite
Colombia

0991
Wonksite
Colombia

0983

0984

0986

0987

0988

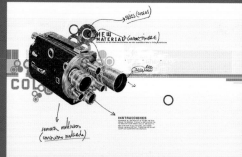

0989

0990

0991

WIE KAHEN SIE ZUM DESIGN?

Ich hatte mit 20 eine Ausgabe der italienischen Vogue in der Hand, doppelt so dick wie die deutsche Ausgabe und voller interessanter Bilder. Das hat einen verborgenen Code in mir aktiviert und mir war sofort klar, ich wollte auch so etwas machen: Images kreieren.

0992	0993	0994		0995	0996	0997		0998	0999	1000	296/297
Dulude	**Dulude**	**Why Not**		**Dulude**	**Dulude**	**Why Not**		**Dulude**	**Dulude**	**Why Not**	**1000**
Canada	Canada	**Associates**		Canada	Canada	**Associates**		Canada	Canada	**Associates**	**3D+**
		UK				UK				UK	**outdoor**
											digital +

0992

0995

0998

0993

0996

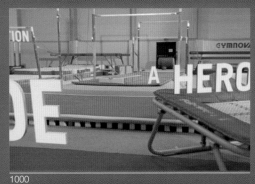

0999

0994

0997

1000

Index.

Atelier Works

0893
Art Director
Ian Chilvers
Designer
Joseph Luffman
Client
Slade Gardens
Software/Hardware
QuarkXPress
Font
Champion

Aufuldish & Warinner

0085
Designer
Bob Aufuldish
Client
California College of the Arts
Software/Hardware
Adobe Illustrator, Adobe Photoshop
Paper/Materials
Titan Dull White Book

0101
Art Director
Bob Aufuldish
Designer
Bob Aufuldish
Client
California College of Arts and Crafts
Software/Hardware
Adobe Illustrator, Adobe Photoshop
Fonts
New Century Schoolbook, Interstate

0143
Art Director
Bob Aufuldish
Designer
Bob Aufuldish
Client
California College of Arts and Crafts
Software/Hardware
Adobe Illustrator, Adobe Photoshop
Fonts
VAG Rounded, Vendetta, Clarendon

0741
Art Director
Bob Aufuldish
Designer
Bob Aufuldish
Client
University of Denver Victoria H. Myhren Gallery
Software/Hardware
Adobe InDesign
Fonts
Bulmer, Latin MT, Clarendon, Bodoni Poster, Bodoni, Egyptian Shadow, Gothic Round, Champion

0742
Art Director
Bob Aufuldish
Designer
Bob Aufuldish

Client
University of Denver Victoria H. Myhren Gallery
Software/Hardware
Adobe InDesign
Fonts
Bulmer, Latin MT, Clarendon, Bodoni Poster, Bodoni, Egyptian Shadow, Gothic Round, Champion

BBK Studio

0658
Art Directors
Steve Frykholm, Yang Kim
Designers
Yang Kim, Michele Chartier
Client
Herman Miller
Software/Hardware
QuarkXPress, Adobe Photoshop
Font
Avenir

0667
Art Director
Yang Kim
Designer
Yang Kim
Client
Jack Ridl
Software/Hardware
QuarkXPress
Font
Humanist

Be Design

0396
Art Director
Eric Read
Designer
Deborah Smith Read
Client
Karma Creations
Software/Hardware
Adobe Illustrator
Font
Customized

Beautiful

0748
Art Director
Kerry Roper
Designer
Kerry Roper
Client
Plinko
Software/Hardware
Adobe Photoshop, Adobe Illustrator
Font
Tsjecho

0751
Art Director
Kerry Roper
Designer
Kerry Roper
Client
Universal Records/Mercury Records
Software/Hardware
Adobe Photoshop, Adobe Illustrator
Font
Mesquite

0752
Art Director
Kerry Roper
Designer
Kerry Roper
Client
Beautiful
Software/Hardware
Adobe Photoshop, Adobe Illustrator
Font
Avenir

0753
Art Director
Kerry Roper
Designer
Kerry Roper
Client
The Big Issue
Software/Hardware
Adobe Photoshop, Adobe Illustrator
Font
Hand drawn (in chocolate)

0754
Art Director
Kerry Roper
Designer
Kerry Roper
Client
Bulgaria Magazine
Software/Hardware
Adobe Photoshop, Adobe Illustrator
Fonts
Temp Mono, hand drawn

0755
Art Director
Kerry Roper
Designer
Kerry Roper
Client
Net Magazine
Software/Hardware
Adobe Photoshop, Adobe Illustrator
Font
Hand drawn

0756
Art Director
Kerry Roper
Designer
Kerry Roper
Client
The Big Issue
Software/Hardware
Adobe Photoshop, Adobe Illustrator
Font
Hand drawn

0757
Art Director
Kerry Roper
Designer
Kerry Roper
Client
Onboard Magazine
Software/Hardware
Adobe Photoshop, Adobe Illustrator
Font
Gold Rush, Mesquite

Belyea

0977
Art Director
Patricia Belyea
Designer
Naomi Murphy
Client
Imperial Lithograph

Software/Hardware
Adobe Illustrator
Paper/Materials
Westvaco, Sterling Ultra, Dull 100C for wrap and calendar pages
Font
Hand drawn

Bisqit Design

0044
Art Director
Daphne Diamant
Designer
Michael Morgan
Client
Bisqit Design
Software/Hardware
QuarkXPress
Font
Helvetaica Neue (Italic)

Blackletter Design Inc.

0237
Art Directors
Ken Bessie, Rick Sealock
Designer
Ken Bessie
Client
Rick Sealock Piglet Press
Software/Hardware
QuarkXPress, Adobe Illustrator, Adobe Photoshop

0268
Art Directors
Ken Bessie, Rick Sealock
Designer
Ken Bessie
Client
Rick Sealock Piglet Press
Software/Hardware
QuarkXPress, Adobe Illustrator, Adobe Photoshop

0269
Art Directors
Ken Bessie, Rick Sealock
Designer
Ken Bessie
Client
Rick Sealock Piglet Press
Software/Hardware
QuarkXPress, Adobe Illustrator, Adobe Photoshop

0270
Art Directors
Ken Bessie, Rick Sealock
Designer
Ken Bessie
Client
Rick Sealock Piglet Press
Software/Hardware
QuarkXPress, Adobe Illustrator, Adobe Photoshop

0271
Art Directors
Ken Bessie, Rick Sealock
Designer
Ken Bessie
Client
Rick Sealock Piglet Press
Software/Hardware
QuarkXPress, Adobe Illustrator, Adobe Photoshop

0272
Art Directors
Ken Bessie, Rick Sealock
Designer
Ken Bessie
Client
Rick Sealock Piglet Press
Software/Hardware
QuarkXPress, Adobe Illustrator, Adobe Photoshop

0273/0274
Art Directors
Ken Bessie, Rick Sealock
Designer
Ken Bessie
Client
Rick Sealock Piglet Press
Software/Hardware
QuarkXPress, Adobe Illustrator, Adobe Photoshop

Blok Design

0022
Art Director
Vanessa Eckstein
Designer
Vanessa Eckstein
Client
The Nienkatver Store

0050
Art Director
Vanessa Eckstein
Designers
Vanessa Eckstein, Frances Chen
Client
RGD/Ontario
Software/Hardware
Adobe Illustrator
Paper/Materials
Cougar

0052
Art Director
Vanessa Eckstein
Designers
Vanessa Eckstein, Frances Chen
Client
RGD/Ontario
Software/Hardware
Adobe Illustrator
Paper/Materials
Cougar

0060
Art Director
Vanessa Eckstein
Designers
Vanessa Eckstein, Frances Chen
Client
RGD/Ontario

Software/Hardware
Adobe Illustrator
Paper/Materials
Cougar

0414
Art Director
Vanessa Eckstein
Designer
Vanessa Eckstein
Client
Distrito Films

0419
Art Director
Vanessa Eckstein
Designers
Vanessa Eckstein, Frances Chen, Stephanie Young
Client
The Production Kitchen
Software/Hardware
Adobe Illustrator
Paper/Materials
Beckett Expression

0443
Art Director
Vanessa Eckstein
Designers
Vanessa Eckstein, Mariana Congegni
Client
Centro

0470
Art Director
Vanessa Eckstein
Designer
Vanessa Eckstein
Client
Distrito Films

0474
Art Director
Vanessa Eckstein
Designers
Vanessa Eckstein, Frances Chen
Client
El Zanson
Software/Hardware
Adobe Illustrator
Paper/Materials
Strathmore Ultimate White

0479
Art Director
Vanessa Eckstein
Designers
Vanessa Eckstein, Mariana Congegni
Client
Centro

0482
Art Director
Vanessa Eckstein
Designers
Vanessa Eckstein, Frances Chen, Stephanie Young
Client
Blok Design
Software/Hardware
Adobe Illustrator

0531
Art Director
Vanessa Eckstein
Designers
Vanessa Eckstein, Mariana Contegni
Client
Ni're Mexico

0532
Art Director
Vanessa Eckstein
Designers
Vanessa Eckstein, Mariana Contegni
Client
Ni're Mexico

0533
Art Director
Vanessa Eckstein
Designers
Vanessa Eckstein, Mariana Contegni
Client
Ni're Mexico

0534
Art Director
Vanessa Eckstein
Designers
Vanessa Eckstein, Mariana Contegni
Client
Ni're Mexico

0803
Art Director
Vanessa Eckstein
Designers
Vanessa Eckstein, Mariana Contegni
Client
Centro

Blue River

0496
Art Director
James Askham
Designer
James Askham
Client
Baltic Centre for Contemporary Art
Software/Hardware
QuarkXPress
Fonts
Akzidenz Grotesk, Baltic Affisch

0605
Art Director
James Askham
Designer
James Askham
Client
Baltic Centre for Contemporary Art
Software/Hardware
QuarkXPress
Fonts
Akzidenz Grotesk, Baltic Affisch

Bright Pink

0069
Art Director
Jessica Glastor
Designers
Jessica Glastor, Carolyn Knight
Client
Bright Pink
Software/Hardware
Adobe Illustrator

Bruketa & Zinic

0226
Art Directors
Davor Bruketa, Nikola Zinic

Designers
**Davor Bruketa,
Nikola Zinić**
Client
Podravka dd.
Software/Hardware
**Freehand, Adobe
Photoshop**
Paper/Materials
Agripina

0597
Art Directors
**Davor Bruketa,
Nikola Zinić**
Designers
**Davor Bruketa,
Nikola Zinić**
Client
Podravka dd.
Software/Hardware
**Freehand,
QuarkXPress**
Font
Tribeca

0599
Art Directors
**Davor Bruketa,
Nikola Zinić**
Designers
**Davor Bruketa,
Nikola Zinić**
Client
Podravka dd.
Software/Hardware
**Freehand,
QuarkXPress**
Font
Tribeca

0708
Art Directors
**Davor Bruketa,
Nikola Zinić**
Designers
**Davor Bruketa,
Nikola Zinić**
Client
Podravka dd.
Software/Hardware
**Freehand,
QuarkXPress**
Font
Tribeca

0916
Art Director
Miran Tomicic
Designer
Miran Tomicic
Client
TDR
Software/Hardware
Adobe Illustrator
Font
Akzidenz Grotesk

Cahan &
Associates
0088
Art Directors
**Bill Cahan,
Bob Dinetz**
Designer
Bob Dinetz
Client
Cahan & Associates

0297/0302
Art Directors
**Bill Cahan,
Kevin Roberson,
Bob Dinetz**
Designers
**Bob Dinetz,
Mark Giglio,
Kevin Roberson**

Client
**StoraEnso/
Consolidated
Papers**
Software/Hardware
**QuarkXPress,
Adobe Photoshop,
Adobe Illustrator**
Paper/Materials
Reflections silk

0524
Art Directors
**Bill Cahan,
Bob Dinetz**
Designer
Bob Dinetz
Client
BRE
Software/Hardware
**QuarkXPress,
Adobe Illustrator,
Adobe Photoshop**
Fonts
**Univers,
Cooper Black**

0535
Art Directors
**Bill Cahan,
Bob Dinetz**
Designer
Bob Dinetz
Client
Alcon Laboratories
Software/Hardware
**QuarkXPress,
Adobe Photoshop,
Adobe Illustrator**
Font
Helvetica

0536
Art Directors
**Bill Cahan,
Bob Dinetz**
Designer
Bob Dinetz
Client
Alcon Laboratories
Software/Hardware
**QuarkXPress,
Adobe Photoshop,
Adobe Illustrator**
Font
Helvetica

0559
Art Director
Bridget Lawrence

0560
Art Director
Bridget Lawrence

0561
Art Director
Bridget Lawrence

0562
Art Director
Bridget Lawrence

0563
Art Director
Bridget Lawrence

0591
Art Director
Bill Cahan
Designer
Todd Simmons
Client
**Linear Technology
Corp.**
Software/Hardware
**Adobe Illustrator,
QuarkXPress**

Paper/Materials
**Kromkote,
Utopia 2 Dull**

0595/0612
Art Directors
**Bill Cahan,
Michael Braley**
Designer
Michael Braley
Client
Maxygen
Font
**Helvetica Neue
(Bold)**

0613
Art Director
Bill Cahan
Designer
Todd Simnons
Client
Silicon Valley Bank
Software/Hardware
**QuarkXPress,
Adobe Illustrator**
Fonts
**Trade Gothic,
Champion Gothic**

0622
Art Director
Bill Cahan
Designer
Todd Simnons
Client
Fogdog Sports
Software/Hardware
**QuarkXPress,
Adobe Illustrator**
Font
Helvetica Neue

0623
Art Director
Bridget Lawrence

0624
Art Director
Bill Cahan
Designer
Todd Simnons
Client
Fogdog Sports
Software/Hardware
**QuarkXPress,
Adobe Illustrator**
Font
Helvetica Neue

0654
Art Directors
**Bill Cahan,
Sharrie Brooks**
Designer
Sharrie Brooks
Client
Valentis
Software/Hardware
**QuarkXPress,
Adobe Illustrator,
Adobe Photoshop**
Paper/Materials
**Cougar Opaque
Vellum**

0655
Art Directors
**Bill Cahan,
Michael Braley**
Designer
Michael Braley
Client
Neoform, Inc.
Software/Hardware
**QuarkXPress,
Adobe Illustrator,
Adobe Photoshop**
Font
Akzidenz Grotesk

0710
Art Director
Bridget Lawrence

0713
Art Director
Bridget Lawrence

0747
Art Director
Bill Cahan
Designer
Todd Simmons
Client
**Linear Technology
Corp.**
Software/Hardware
**Adobe Illustrator,
QuarkXPress**
Paper/Materials
**Kromkote,
Utopia 2 Dull**

Capaekel
0382
Art Director
Ricardo Fernandes
Designer
Tania Carvallro
Client
RDP — Antena 2
Software/Hardware
Freehand
Fonts
**Bodoni, Meta,
Helvetica**

0452
Art Director
Ricardo Fernandes
Designer
**Patricia Salatar
Rimr**
Client
RDP — Antena 2
Software/Hardware
**Freehand,
Adobe Photoshop**
Fonts
**Meta, Univers,
Times**

0485
Art Director
Ricardo Fernandes
Designer
**Patricia Salatar
Rimr**
Client
RDP — Antena 2
Software/Hardware
**Freehand,
Adobe Photoshop**
Fonts
**Meta, Univers,
Times**

0488
Art Director
Ricardo Fernandes
Designer
Tania Carvallro
Client
RDP — Antena 2
Software/Hardware
Freehand
Fonts
**Bodoni, Meta,
Helvetica**

Capsule
0377
Designer
Brian Adducci
Client
Euclue Technologies

Software/Hardware
Adobe Illustrator
Font
Din

0387
Designer
Dan Bagoenstoss
Client
**Society of American
Fight Directors**
Software/Hardware
Adobe Illustrator
Fonts
**Hoefler Ziggurat,
Knockout**

0388
Designer
Dan Bagoenstoss
Client
**Society of American
Fight Directors**
Software/Hardware
Adobe Illustrator
Fonts
**Hoefler Ziggurat,
Knockout**

0689
Designers
**Greg Brose, Dan
Bagoenstoss, Brian
Adducci, Anchalle
Chambundagonse**
Software/Hardware
**QuarkXPress,
Adobe Illustrator,
Adobe Photoshop**
Fonts
**Trade Gothic
(extended),
Clearface**

0711
Designer
Greg Brose
Client
**Belcorp Financial
Group**
Software/Hardware
Adobe InDesign

0843
Designer
Brian Adducci
Client
Lindquist & Vennum
Software/Hardware
Adobe Illustrator
Font
Akzidenz Grotesk

0844
Designer
Brian Adducci
Client
Lindquist & Vennum
Software/Hardware
Adobe Illustrator
Font
Akzidenz Grotesk

0876
Designer
Greg Brose
Client
Trend Agenda
Software/Hardware
Adobe Illustrator
Fonts
**Font Bureau Miller,
Hoefler Champion
Gothic**

0944
Designer
Brian Adducci

Client
I FLY
Software/Hardware
**Adobe Illustrator,
Excentro**
Fonts
**Akzidenz Grotesk,
Test Pilot, Collective
Ultra Magnetic**

Carter
Wong
Tomlin
0150
Art Director
Phil Carter
Designer
Phil Carter
Client
Jake Scott
Software/Hardware
Letterpress

0805
Art Director
Phil Wong
Designer
Clare Wigg
Client
Royal Mail
Software/Hardware
Adobe Illustrator

0807
Art Director
Phil Wong
Designer
Clare Wigg
Client
Royal Mail
Software/Hardware
Adobe Illustrator
Font
Chevin

0950
Art Director
Phil Carter
Designer
Phil Carter
Illustrator/Calligrapher
Brian Cairns
Client
Jake Scott
Fonts
Hand drawn

CDT
Design
0008
Art Director
Christian Altmann
Designer
Alistair Hall
Client
**The Royal College
of Art**
Software/Hardware
QuarkXPress
Paper/Materials
Imagine, Chromolux

0078
Art Director
Christian Altmann
Designer
Alistair Hall
Client
**The Royal College
of Art**
Software/Hardware
QuarkXPress
Paper/Materials
Imagine, Chromolux

Chen
Design
Associates
0879
Art Director
Joshua C. Chen
Designers
**Max Spector,
Jennifer Tolo**
Client
AIGA
Software/Hardware
**QuarkXPress,
Adobe Illustrator,
Adobe Photoshop**
Paper/Materials
**Fox River
Coronado, Bright
White Vellum,
Gilbert Clearfold
White Light**

Cheng
Design
0767
Designer
Karen Cheng
Client
**Simpson Center for
the Humanities**
Software/Hardware
Adobe Illustrator
Fonts
**Bell Gothic,
Trade Gothic**

0769
Designer
Karen Cheng
Client
**Simpson Center for
the Humanities**
Software/Hardware
Adobe Illustrator
Fonts
**Bell Gothic,
Trade Gothic**

0780
Designer
Karen Cheng
Client
**Simpson Center for
the Humanities**
Software/Hardware
Adobe Illustrator
Fonts
**Bell Gothic,
Trade Gothic**

Chermayeff
& Geismar
Inc.
0929
Designer
Steff Geissbuhler
Client
In-house
Font
Customized

Circle K
Studio
0059
Art Director
Julie Keenan
Designer
Julie Keenan
Client
Circle K Studio

Software/Hardware
Adobe Illustrator
Paper/Materials
Rubber Stamp
Sewn

0102
Art Director
Julie Keenan
Designer
Julie Keenan
Client
Jamie Schulman
Deborah Dalfen
Software/Hardware
Adobe Illustrator
Paper/Materials
Custom Rubber
Stamp

0679
Art Director
Julie Keenan
Designer
Julie Keenan
Client
The University of
Maryland School of
Pharmacy
Software/Hardware
QuarkXPress

Concrete
(Chicago)
0077
Art Director
Jilly Simons
Designers
Jilly Simons,
Regan Todd
Client
Concrete
Software/Hardware
QuarkXPress
Fonts
Dalliance Script,
Franklin Gothic

0084
Art Director
Jilly Simons
Designers
Jilly Simons,
Regan Todd
Client
School of
Architecture,
Washington
University in St.
Louis
Software/Hardware
QuarkXPress
Fonts
Univers (BQ),
Quay Sans

0415
Art Director
Jilly Simons
Designers
Jilly Simons,
Regan Todd
Client
MSP Paris, SAS
Software/Hardware
QuarkXPress,
Adobe Illustrator
Fonts
Univers, hand
drawn (logo)

0635
Art Director
Jilly Simons
Designers
Jilly Simons,
Regan Todd
Client
Hinge

Software/Hardware
QuarkXPress
Fonts
Cochin Grotesque
MT Condensed,
Futura, Avenir,
Letter Gothic, Trade
Gothic, Univers,
Univers Condensed

0636
Art Director
Jilly Simons
Designers
Jilly Simons,
Regan Todd
Client
Hinge
Software/Hardware
QuarkXPress
Fonts
Cochin Grotesque
MT Condensed,
Futura, Avenir,
Letter Gothic, Trade
Gothic, Univers,
Univers Condensed

Crush
Design
0140
Art Director
Chris Pelling
Designer
Chris Pelling
Client
Camron PR
Software/Hardware
Adobe Photoshop,
Adobe Illustrator,
QuarkXPress

0331
Art Director
Carl Rush
Designer
Carl Rush
Client
Harvill Publishing
Software/Hardware
Adobe Illustrator,
Adobe Photoshop
Paper/Materials
Matt Lamiate,
emboss

0453
Art Director
Carl Rush
Designer
Carl Rush
Client
Wea Records
Software/Hardware
Adobe Illustrator

0454
Art Director
Carl Rush
Designer
Chris Pelling
Client
William Grant &
Sons
Software/Hardware
Adobe Illustrator

0455
Art Director
Carl Rush
Designer
Carl Rush
Client
Palm Pictures
Software/Hardware
Adobe Photoshop
Paper/Materials
Paper, scissors

0456
Art Director
Carl Rush
Designer
Carl Rush
Client
Palm Pictures
Software/Hardware
Adobe Illustrator

0457
Art Director
Carl Rush
Designer
Simon Scater
Client
William Grant &
Sons
Software/Hardware
Adobe Illustrator

0458
Art Director
Carl Rush
Designer
Simon Scater
Client
Heineken Int.
Software/Hardware
Adobe Illustrator

0459
Art Director
Carl Rush
Designer
Simon Scater
Client
William Grant &
Sons
Software/Hardware
Adobe Illustrator

0460
Art Director
Carl Rush
Designer
Tim Diacon
Client
Heineken
International
Software/Hardware
Adobe Illustrator

0486
Art Director
Carl Rush
Designer
Tim Diacon
Client
Splendid
Communications
Software/Hardware
Adobe Illustrator

0845
Art Director
Carl Rush
Designer
Carl Rush
Client
Self Promotion
Software/Hardware
Adobe Photoshop

0865
Art Director
Carl Rush
Designer
Tim Diacon
Client
The Music Matrix
Software/Hardware
Adobe Photoshop

0868
Art Director
Carl Rush
Designer
Tim Diacon

Client
The Music Matrix
Software/Hardware
Adobe Photoshop

0912
Art Director
Carl Rush
Designer
Simon Scater
Client
Playlab/Toy2r
Paper/Materials
Spray paint, letraset

0937
Art Director
Carl Rush
Designer
Chris Pelling
Client
Full on Films
Software/Hardware
Adobe Illustrator,
Adobe Photoshop,
Adobe After Effects

0939
Art Director
Carl Rush
Designer
Carl Rush
Client
Palm Pictures
Software/Hardware
Adobe Photoshop
Paper/Materials
Photocopier

0945
Art Director
Carl Rush
Designer
Carl Rush
Client
Palm Pictures
Software/Hardware
Adobe Photoshop

0971
Art Director
Carl Rush
Designer
Chris Pelling
Client
Full on Films
Software/Hardware
Adobe Illustrator,
Adobe Photoshop,
Adobe After Effects

Danielle
Foushee
Design
0371
Art Director
Danielle Foushee
Designer
Danielle Foushee
Client
Danielle Foushee
Software/Hardware
Adobe Illustrator,
Adobe InDesign

David
Salafia/
Laura
Salafia
0051
Art Directors
David Salafia,
Laura Salafia

Designers
David Salafia,
Laura Salafia
Client
David Salafia,
Laura Salafia
Software/Hardware
QuarkXPress
Fonts
Mantinia, Mrs Eaves

Design
Center
0765
Art Director
Eduard Cehovin
Designer
Eduard Cehovin
Client
One Man-Show on
Billboard
Software/Hardware
Adobe Illustrator

0858
Art Director
Eduard Cehovin
Designer
Eduard Cehovin
Client
One Man-Show on
Billboard
Software/Hardware
Adobe Illustrator

0874
Art Director
Eduard Cehovin
Designer
Eduard Cehovin
Client
One Man-Show on
Billboard
Software/Hardware
Adobe Illustrator

Design
Depot
Creative
Bureau
0627
Art Director
Petr Bankov
Designer
Petr Bankov
Client
Design Depot

0628
Art Director
Petr Bankov
Designer
Petr Bankov
Client
Design Depot

0629
Art Director
Petr Bankov
Designer
Petr Bankov
Client
Design Depot

Design
hoch drei
GmbH &
Co. KG
0739
Art Directors
Wolfram Schaeffer,
Marcus Wichmann

Designer
Marcus Wichmann
Client
Dairyler Chrysler
AG
Software/Hardware
QuarkXPress,
Freehand, Adobe
Photoshop
Font
Corporate S

D-Fuse
0035
Art Director
Mike Faulkner
Designer
Mike Faulkner
Client
D-Fuse
Software/Hardware
Adobe Photoshop,
Freehand
Font
Franklin

0042
Art Director
Mike Faulkner
Designer
Mike Faulkner
Client
D-Fuse
Software/Hardware
Adobe Photoshop,
Freehand

0043
Art Director
Mike Faulkner
Designer
Mike Faulkner
Client
D-Fuse
Software/Hardware
Adobe Photoshop,
Freehand

0090
Art Director
Mike Faulkner
Designer
Mike Faulkner
Client
D-Fuse
Software/Hardware
Adobe Photoshop,
Freehand

Dovetail
Communi-
cations,
Hartford
Design,
Woz
Design
0523
Art Directors
Ted Stoir,
Tim Hartford,
David Wozniak
Designers
Ted Stoir,
Tim Hartford,
David Wozniak
Client
Underwriters
Laboratories
Software/Hardware
Adobe InDesign,
Adobe Illustrator,
Adobe Photoshop
Font
Akzidenz Grotesk

Duffy
Singapore
0189
Art Director
Christopher Lee
Designer
Christopher Lee
Client
Designers
Association
Singapore
Software/Hardware
Freehand, Adobe
Photoshop
Font
Trade Gothic

0224
Art Director
Christopher Lee
Designer
Christopher Lee
Client
Designers
Association
Singapore
Software/Hardware
Freehand, Adobe
Photoshop

0522
Art Director
Christopher Lee
Designer
Christopher Lee
Client
Wizards of Light
Software/Hardware
Freehand, Adobe
Photoshop
Fonts
Avant Garde Gothic,
Courier, Mrs Eaves,
Times

0609
Art Director
Christopher Lee
Designers
Christopher Lee,
Cara, Kai, Larry,
Welping, Michelle
Software/Hardware
Freehand, Adobe
Photoshop
Font
Trade Gothic

0616
Art Director
Christopher Lee
Designers
Christopher Lee,
Cara, Kai, Larry,
Welping, Michelle
Software/Hardware
Freehand, Adobe
Photoshop
Font
Trade Gothic

0660
Art Director
Christopher Lee
Designer
Christopher Lee
Client
Wizards of Light
Software/Hardware
Freehand, Adobe
Photoshop

0714
Art Director
Christopher Lee
Designer
Christopher Lee

Client
Wizards of Light
Software/Hardware
Freehand, Adobe
Photoshop

Dulude

0071
Art Director
Denis Dulude
Designer
Denis Dulude
Client
Denis Dulude
Software/Hardware
Adobe Illustrator,
Adobe Photoshop,
iTunes
Fonts
Dulude/Magma,
Diesel (2 Rebels)

0483
Art Director
Denis Dulude
Designer
Denis Dulude
Client
Denis Dulude
Software/Hardware
Adobe Illustrator,
Adobe Photoshop,
FontLab

0544
Art Director
Denis Dulude
Designer
Denis Dulude
Client
Pol Baril
Software/Hardware
Adobe InDesign,
Adobe Illustrator,
iTunes

0545
Art Director
Denis Dulude
Designer
Denis Dulude
Client
Pol Baril
Software/Hardware
Adobe InDesign,
Adobe Illustrator,
iTunes
Font
Times (customized)

0546
Art Director
Denis Dulude
Designer
Denis Dulude
Client
Pol Baril
Software/Hardware
Adobe InDesign,
Adobe Illustrator,
iTunes
Font
Times (customized)

0547
Art Director
Denis Dulude
Designer
Denis Dulude
Client
Pol Baril
Software/Hardware
Adobe InDesign,
Adobe Illustrator,
iTunes

0548
Art Director
Denis Dulude

Designer
Denis Dulude
Client
Pol Baril
Software/Hardware
Adobe InDesign,
Adobe Illustrator,
iTunes
Font
Times (customized)

0549
Art Director
Denis Dulude
Designer
Denis Dulude
Client
Pol Baril
Software/Hardware
Adobe InDesign,
Adobe Illustrator,
iTunes
Font
Times (customized)

0550
Art Director
Denis Dulude
Designer
Denis Dulude
Client
Pol Baril
Software/Hardware
Adobe InDesign,
Adobe Illustrator,
iTunes
Font
Times (customized)

0551
Art Director
Denis Dulude
Designer
Denis Dulude
Client
Pol Baril
Software/Hardware
Adobe InDesign,
Adobe Illustrator,
iTunes

0552
Art Director
Denis Dulude
Designer
Denis Dulude
Client
Pol Baril
Software/Hardware
Adobe InDesign,
Adobe Illustrator,
iTunes

0553
Art Director
Denis Dulude
Designer
Denis Dulude
Client
Pol Baril
Software/Hardware
Adobe InDesign,
Adobe Illustrator,
iTunes

0554
Art Director
Denis Dulude
Designer
Denis Dulude
Client
Pol Baril
Software/Hardware
Adobe InDesign,
Adobe Illustrator,

0555
Art Director
Denis Dulude
Designer
Denis Dulude
Client
Pol Baril
Software/Hardware
Adobe InDesign,
Adobe Illustrator,
iTunes

0678
Art Director
Denis Dulude
Designer
Denis Dulude
Client
Pol Baril
Software/Hardware
Adobe InDesign,
Adobe Illustrator,
iTunes

0696
Art Director
Denis Dulude
Designer
Denis Dulude
Client
Choiniere
Photographe
Software/Hardware
Adobe InDesign,
Adobe Illustrator
Font
Trade Gothic
(customized)

0770
Art Director
Denis Dulude
Designer
Denis Dulude
Client
Denis Dulude
Software/Hardware
Adobe Illustrator,
Adobe Photoshop,
iTunes

0771
Art Director
Denis Dulude
Designer
Denis Dulude
Client
Denis Dulude
Software/Hardware
Adobe Illustrator,
Adobe Photoshop,
iTunes

0774
Art Director
Denis Dulude
Designer
Denis Dulude
Client
Denis Dulude
Software/Hardware
Adobe Illustrator,
Adobe Photoshop,
iTunes

0841
Art Director
Denis Dulude
Designer
Denis Dulude
Client
Denis Dulude
Software/Hardware
Adobe Illustrator,
Adobe Photoshop,
iTunes

0875
Art Director
Denis Dulude
Designer
Denis Dulude
Client
Denis Dulude
Software/Hardware
Adobe Illustrator,
Adobe Photoshop,
iTunes

0992
Art Director
Denis Dulude
Designer
Denis Dulude
Client
Cité-Amerique
Software/Hardware
Adobe InDesign,
Adobe After Effects
Font
Trade Gothic
(customized)

0993
Art Director
Denis Dulude
Designer
Denis Dulude
Client
Cité-Amerique
Software/Hardware
Adobe InDesign,
Adobe After Effects
Font
Trade Gothic
(customized)

0995
Art Director
Denis Dulude
Designer
Denis Dulude
Client
Cité-Amerique
Software/Hardware
Adobe InDesign,
Adobe After Effects
Font
Trade Gothic
(customized)

0996
Art Director
Denis Dulude
Designer
Denis Dulude
Client
Cité-Amerique
Software/Hardware
Adobe InDesign,
Adobe After Effects
Font
Trade Gothic
(customized)

0998
Art Director
Denis Dulude
Designer
Denis Dulude
Client
Cité-Amerique
Software/Hardware
Adobe InDesign,
Adobe After Effects
Font
Trade Gothic
(customized)

0999
Art Director
Denis Dulude
Designer
Denis Dulude
Client
Cité-Amerique

Software/Hardware
Adobe InDesign,
Adobe After Effects
Font
Trade Gothic
(customized)

Dynamo

0073
Art Director
Brian Nolan
Designer
Brian Nolan
Client
Amanda Brady
Software/Hardware
QuarkXPress
Font
Garamond

Eggers &
Diaper

0306
Art Director
Mark Diaper
Designer
Mark Diaper
Client
Artangel/Public Art
Fund

0695
Art Directors
Birgit Eggers,
Mark Diaper
Designers
Birgit Eggers,
Mark Diaper
Client
European Space
Agency

0732
Art Directors
Birgit Eggers,
Mark Diaper
Designers
Birgit Eggers,
Mark Diaper
Client
European Space
Agency

Elizabeth
Resnick
Design

0824
Art Director
Elizabeth Resnick
Designer
Elizabeth Resnick
Client
Massachusetts
College of Art
Software/Hardware
QuarkXPress
Fonts
Martina, Galliard

elliottyoung

0400
Art Director
Dan Elliott
Designer
Dan Elliott
Client
Jet Couture

0463
Art Director
Dan Elliott
Designer
Dan Elliott
Client
Jet Couture

0465
Art Director
Dan Elliott
Designer
Dan Elliott
Client
Jet Couture

emeryfrost

0198
Designer
Emeryfrost
Client
Zembla

0208
Designer
Emeryfrost
Client
Zembla

0233
Designer
Emeryfrost
Client
Zembla

0258
Designer
Emeryfrost
Client
Zembla

0259
Designer
Emeryfrost
Client
Zembla

0261
Designer
Emeryfrost
Client
Zembla

0262
Designer
Emeryfrost
Client
Zembla

0286
Designer
Emeryfrost
Client
Zembla

0305
Designer
Emeryfrost
Client
Zembla

0313
Designer
Emeryfrost
Client
Zembla

0355
Designer
Emeryfrost
Client
Zembla

0357
Designer
Emeryfrost
Client
Zembla

0358
Designer
Emeryfrost
Client
Zembla

0359
Designer
Emeryfrost
Client
Zembla

Enspace,
Inc.

0592
Designers
Jenn Visocky
O'Grady, Ken
Visocky O'Grady,
Paul Perchinske
Client
Solutions At Work
Software/Hardware
QuarkXPress,
Adobe Illustrator,
Adobe Photoshop
Fonts
Franklin Gothic,
Centennial

0593
Designers
Jenn Visocky
O'Grady, Ken
Visocky O'Grady,
Paul Perchinske
Client
Solutions At Work
Software/Hardware
QuarkXPress,
Adobe Illustrator,
Adobe Photoshop
Fonts
Franklin Gothic,
Centennial

0594
Designers
Jenn Visocky
O'Grady, Ken
Visocky O'Grady,
Paul Perchinske
Client
Solutions At Work
Software/Hardware
QuarkXPress,
Adobe Illustrator,
Adobe Photoshop
Fonts
Franklin Gothic,
Centennial

0818
Designers
Jenn Visocky
O'Grady, Ken
Visocky O'Grady,
Paul Perchinske
Client
Cleveland Chamber
Symphony
Software/Hardware
Adobe InDesign,
Adobe Illustrator,
Adobe Photoshop
Font
Trade Gothic

Envision+

0541/0542
Designers
Esther
Mildenberger,
Brian Switzer
Client
20/20 Media
Software/Hardware
Adobe Illustrator,
Adobe Photoshop

0543
Designers
Esther Mildenberger, Brian Switzer
Client
20/20 Media
Software/Hardware
Adobe Illustrator, Adobe Photoshop

0671
Designers
Esther Mildenberger, Brian Switzer
Client
Interaction Design Institute Ivrea
Software/Hardware
QuarkXPress, Adobe Illustrator, Adobe Photoshop
Fonts
FF (sans), Bodoni

0851
Designer
Brian Switzer
Client
Interaction Design Institute Ivrea
Software/Hardware
QuarkXPress, Adobe Photoshop
Fonts
FF (serif), FF Din

Felder Grafikdesign

0520
Art Director
Peter Felder
Designers
Rene Dalpra, Peter Felder
Client
Telefonseelsorge Vorarlberg
Software/Hardware
QuarkXPress
Paper/Materials
Elk Munken Offset, 150 gsm

0659
Art Director
Peter Felder
Client
Felder Grafikdesign
Software/Hardware
QuarkXPress
Paper/Materials
Spoilage, wastepaper

0662
Art Director
Peter Felder
Client
Felder Grafikdesign
Software/Hardware
QuarkXPress
Paper/Materials
Spoilage, wastepaper

0665
Art Director
Peter Felder
Client
Felder Grafikdesign
Software/Hardware
QuarkXPress
Paper/Materials
Spoilage, wastepaper

0666
Art Director
Peter Felder
Client
Felder Grafikdesign
Software/Hardware
QuarkXPress
Paper/Materials
Spoilage, wastepaper

Felton Communi-cation

0895
Art Director
Brian Furnell
Client
Terrence Higgins Trust
Software/Hardware
QuarkXPress, Adobe Photoshop
Paper/Materials
Challenger Offset, vinyl

0899
Art Director
Brian Furnell
Client
Terrence Higgins Trust
Software/Hardware
QuarkXPress, Adobe Photoshop
Paper/Materials
Challenger Offset, vinyl

0924
Art Director
Brian Furnell
Client
Terrence Higgins Trust
Software/Hardware
QuarkXPress, Adobe Photoshop
Paper/Materials
Challenger Offset, vinyl

Christine Fent, Manja Uellpap, Gilmar Wendt

0018
Art Directors
Christine Fent, Manja Uellpap, Gilmar Wendt
Designers
Christine Fent, Manja Uellpap, Gilmar Wendt
Client
ISTD
Software/Hardware
QuarkXPress
Fonts
Architype Tschichold, Augustea

0020
Art Directors
Christine Fent, Manja Uellpap, Gilmar Wendt
Designers
Christine Fent, Manja Uellpap, Gilmar Wendt
Client
ISTD
Software/Hardware
QuarkXPress
Fonts
Architype Tschichold, Augustea

Form Fünf Bremen

0036
Designer
Daniel Henry Bastian
Client
Form Fünf Bremen
Software/Hardware
Freehand

Marino A. Gallo

0386
Client
Polestar
Software/Hardware
Adobe Illustrator, Adobe Photoshop

0389
Client
Marino A. Gallo
Software/Hardware
Adobe Illustrator, Adobe Photoshop

0464
Client
Marino A. Gallo
Software/Hardware
Adobe Illustrator, Adobe Photoshop

0967
Client
Ogilvy & Mather
Software/Hardware
Adobe Illustrator, Adobe Photoshop

Gee & Chung Design

0637
Art Director
Earl Gee
Designers
Earl Gee, Fani Chung
Client
DCM-Doll Capital Management
Software/Hardware
Adobe InDesign, Adobe Illustrator, Adobe Photoshop
Fonts
Adobe Garamond, Trade Gothic

Gervais

0759
Art Director
Fran Gois Gervais
Designer
Fran Gois Gervais
Client
Fran Gois Gervais
Software/Hardware
Adobe Photoshop

0794
Art Director
Jacqueline VD Brugge
Designer
Jacqueline VD Brugge
Client
In Discussion Right Now (publisher)

0798
Art Director
Gervais
Designer
Gervais
Client
Papyrus Paper Company NC

Ash Gibson

0229
Art Director
Ash Gibson
Designer
Ash Gibson
Client
Dennis Publishing (UK)
Software/Hardware
Adobe Illustrator, Adobe Photoshop
Font
FJ Extended (by Ash Gibson)

0310
Art Director
Ash Gibson
Designer
Ash Gibson
Client
Dennis Publishing (UK)
Software/Hardware
Adobe Illustrator, Adobe Photoshop
Font
FJ Extended (by Ash Gibson)

0311
Art Director
Ash Gibson
Designer
Ash Gibson
Client
Dennis Publishing (UK)
Software/Hardware
Adobe Illustrator, Adobe Photoshop
Font
FJ Extended (by Ash Gibson)

0346
Art Director
Ash Gibson
Designer
Ash Gibson
Client
Dennis Publishing (UK)
Software/Hardware
Adobe Illustrator, Adobe Photoshop
Font
FJ Extended (by Ash Gibson)

Giorgio Davanzo Design

0471
Art Director
Giorgio Davanzo
Designer
Giorgio Davanzo
Client
PD3
Software/Hardware
QuarkXPress, Adobe Illustrator
Font
Franklin Gothic

Gouthier Design Inc.

0089
Art Director
Jonathan Gouthier
Designers
Jonathan Gouthier, Kiley Del Valle
Client
Gouthier Design
Software/Hardware
Adobe Photoshop, Adobe Illustrator, QuarkXPress
Paper/Materials
French Construction, Stora Enso Centura

0171
Art Director
Jonathan Gouthier
Designers
Jonathan Gouthier, Kiley Del Valle
Client
Gouthier Design
Software/Hardware
Adobe Photoshop, Adobe Illustrator, QuarkXPress
Paper/Materials
French Construction, Stora Enso Centura

0473
Art Director
Jonathan Gouthier
Designers
Jonathan Gouthier, Kiley Del Valle
Client
Gouthier Design
Software/Hardware
Adobe Photoshop, Adobe Illustrator, QuarkXPress
Paper/Materials
French Construction, Stora Enso Centura

0731
Art Director
Jonathan Gouthier
Designers
Jonathan Gouthier, Kiley Del Valle
Client
Ad Fed of Greater Fort Lauderdale
Software/Hardware
Adobe Illustrator, Adobe Photoshop
Font
FJ Extended (by Ash Gibson)

Graphiculture

0001
Art Director
Chad Olson
Client
Ann E. Cutting
Software/Hardware
QuarkXPress
Font
Clarendon

0005
Art Director
Chad Olson
Client
Ann E. Cutting
Software/Hardware
QuarkXPress
Font
Clarendon

0183
Art Director
Chad Olson
Client
Ann E. Cutting
Software/Hardware
QuarkXPress
Font
Clarendon

Groothuis & Malsy

0222
Art Directors
Victor Maisy, Gilmar Wendt
Designer
Gilmar Wendt
Client
Groothuis & Malsy
Software/Hardware
QuarkXPress
Paper/Materials
Schleipen Fly, Rainbow Rosebud

0227
Art Directors
Victor Maisy, Gilmar Wendt
Designer
Gilmar Wendt
Client
Groothuis & Malsy
Software/Hardware
QuarkXPress
Paper/Materials
Schleipen Fly, Rainbow Rosebud

0263
Art Directors
Victor Maisy, Gilmar Wendt
Designer
Gilmar Wendt
Client
Groothuis & Malsy
Software/Hardware
QuarkXPress
Paper/Materials
Schleipen Fly, Rainbow Rosebud

0343
Art Directors
Victor Malsy, Gilmar Wendt
Designer
Gilmar Wendt
Client
Groothuis & Malsy
Software/Hardware
QuarkXPress
Paper/Materials
Schleipen Fly, Rainbow Rosebud

0363
Art Directors
Victor Malsy, Gilmar Wendt
Designer
Gilmar Wendt
Client
Groothuis & Malsy
Software/Hardware
QuarkXPress
Paper/Materials
Schleipen Fly, Rainbow Rosebud

Guru Design

0586
Art Director
Claus Rysser
Designer
Claus Rysser
Client
Guru Design
Software/Hardware
Adobe Photoshop, Adobe Illustrator
Fonts
Helvetica Neue, Haetenschweiller, Verdana

0587
Art Director
Claus Rysser
Designer
Claus Rysser
Client
Guru Design
Software/Hardware
Adobe Photoshop, Adobe Illustrator
Fonts
Helvetica Neue, Haetenschweiller, Verdana

0589
Art Director
Claus Rysser
Designer
Claus Rysser
Client
Guru Design
Software/Hardware
Adobe Photoshop, Adobe Illustrator
Fonts
Helvetica Neue, Haetenschweiller, Verdana

0618
Art Director
Claus Rysser
Designer
Claus Rysser
Client
Guru Design
Software/Hardware
Adobe Photoshop, Adobe Illustrator

Fonts
Helvetica Neue,
Haetenschweiller,
Verdana

0621
Art Director
Claus Rysser
Designer
Claus Rysser
Client
Guru Design
Software/Hardware
Adobe Photoshop,
Adobe Illustrator
Fonts
Helvetica Neue,
Haetenschweiller,
Verdana

0693
Art Director
Claus Rysser
Designer
Claus Rysser
Client
Guru Design
Software/Hardware
Adobe Photoshop,
Adobe Illustrator
Fonts
Helvetica Neue,
Haetenschweiller,
Verdana

H2D2, Visual Communi-cations

0083
Art Director
Markus Remscheid
Client
Self Promotion
Software/Hardware
Freehand,
Adobe Photoshop
Font
H2D2—Flame

Harcus Design

0186
Art Director
Annette Harcus
Designer
Phoebe Besley
Client
John Guthrie
Software/Hardware
Adobe Illustrator,
Adobe Photoshop
Font
Rosewood—Fill

0398
Art Director
Annette Harcus
Designers
Melonie Ryan,
Annette Harcus
Client
Arinya Accessories
Software/Hardware
Adobe Illustrator
Fonts
Futura, hand drawn

0497
Art Director
Annette Harcus
Designer
Marianne Walter

Client
Man Investments
Software/Hardware
Adobe Illustrator,
Adobe Photoshop,
QuarkXPress
Font
Helvetica Neue

0498
Art Director
Annette Harcus
Designer
Marianne Walter
Client
Man Investments
Software/Hardware
Adobe Illustrator,
Adobe Photoshop,
QuarkXPress
Font
Helvetica Neue

0619
Art Director
Annette Harcus
Designers
Melonie Ryan,
Annette Harcus
Client
Yalumba Wine
Company
Software/Hardware
Adobe Illustrator,
Adobe Photoshop,
QuarkXPress
Fonts
Bodoni Antiqua,
Helvetica Neue

0906
Art Director
Annette Harcus
Designer
Phoebe Besley
Client
The Evans Wine
Company
Software/Hardware
Adobe Illustrator,
Adobe Photoshop
Font
Trajan

0909
Art Director
Annette Harcus
Designers
Melonie Ryan,
Annette Harcus
Client
Yalumba Wine
Company
Software/Hardware
Adobe Illustrator
Font
Serlio

Harriman steel

0776
Art Director
Harrimansteel
Designer
Harrimansteel
Client
First Impression Ltd
Software/Hardware
Adobe Illustrator
Fonts
Illustrator Swiss,
Helvetica Neue

0779
Art Director
Harrimansteel
Designer
Harrimansteel

Client
First Impression Ltd
Software/Hardware
Adobe Illustrator
Fonts
Illustrator Swiss,
Helvetica Neue

0782
Art Director
Harrimansteel
Designer
Harrimansteel
Client
First Impression Ltd
Software/Hardware
Adobe Illustrator
Fonts
Illustrator Swiss,
Helvetica Neue

0822
Art Director
Harrimansteel
Designer
Harrimansteel
Client
Hurley International
Paper/Materials
Tracing paper
and pen
Font
Hand drawn

Hartford Design

0369
Art Director
Tim Hartford
Designer
Ron Alikpala
Client
Wishbone
Restaurant
Software/Hardware
QuarkXPress,
Adobe Illustrator,
Adobe Photoshop
Font
Customized

0448
Art Director
Tim Hartford
Designer
Tim Hartford
Client
Hartford Design
Software/Hardware
QuarkXPress,
Adobe Illustrator
Font
Seria Sans

0493
Art Director
Tim Hartford
Designer
Tim Hartford
Client
Jessica Tampas
Photography
Software/Hardware
QuarkXPress,
Adobe Illustrator
Font
OCRA

0525
Art Director
Tim Hartford
Designer
Tim Hartford
Client
Marc Hauser
Photography,
Nimrod Systems

QuarkXPress,
Adobe Illustrator,
Adobe Photoshop
Fonts
Clarendon,
Trade Gothic

0526
Art Director
Tim Hartford
Designer
Ron Alikpala
Client
American Dietetic
Association
Software/Hardware
QuarkXPress,
Adobe Illustrator,
Adobe Photoshop
Fonts
Trade Gothic,
Adobe Garamond

0530
Art Director
Tim Hartford
Designer
Tim Hartford
Client
Jessica Tampas
Photography
Software/Hardware
QuarkXPress,
Adobe Illustrator

0588
Art Director
Tim Hartford
Designer
Tim Hartford
Client
Marc Hauser
Photography,
Nimrod Systems
Software/Hardware
QuarkXPress,
Adobe Illustrator,
Adobe Photoshop

0614
Art Director
Tim Hartford
Designer
Tim Hartford
Client
American Dietetic
Association
Software/Hardware
QuarkXPress,
Adobe Illustrator,
Adobe Photoshop
Fonts
Helvetica Neue

0630
Art Director
Tim Hartford
Designer
Tim Hartford
Client
Marc Hauser
Photography,
Nimrod Systems
Software/Hardware
QuarkXPress,
Adobe Illustrator,
Adobe Photoshop

0632
Art Director
Tim Hartford
Designer
Tim Hartford
Client
Marc Hauser
Photography,
Nimrod Systems

QuarkXPress,
Adobe Illustrator,
Adobe Photoshop

0675
Art Director
Tim Hartford
Designer
Tim Hartford
Client
American Dietetic
Association
Software/Hardware
QuarkXPress,
Adobe Illustrator,
Adobe Photoshop

0728
Art Director
Tim Hartford
Designer
Tim Hartford
Client
Bill Tucker,
Nimrod Systems
Software/Hardware
QuarkXPress,
Adobe Photoshop
Font
Trade Gothic

Heckman

0098
Art Director
Denise Heckman
Designer
Denise Heckman
Client
Syracuse University
Software/Hardware
QuarkXPress,
Adobe Photoshop,
Adobe Illustrator
Fonts
Akzidenz Grotesk,
Garamond

0100
Art Director
Denise Heckman
Designer
Denise Heckman
Client
Syracuse University
Software/Hardware
QuarkXPress,
Adobe Photoshop,
Adobe Illustrator
Fonts
Andale Mono,
Akzidenz Grotesk,
Times

Hornall Anderson Design Works, Inc.

0424
Art Directors
James Tee,
John Anicker
Designers
James Tee,
Elmer dela Cruz,
Kris Delaney
Client
Zango
Software/Hardware
Freehand

0436
Art Director
Jack Anderson

Designers
Gretchen Cook,
Kathy Saito
Client
TruckTrax
Software/Hardware
Freehand

0565
Art Director
Jack Anderson
Designers
Jack Anderson,
Andrew Wicklund,
Mark Popich, Henry
Yiu, Lauren
DiRusso, Ed Lee
Client
Seattle
SuperSonics
Software/Hardware
QuarkXPress,
Adobe Photoshop

0566
Art Director
Jack Anderson
Designers
Jack Anderson,
Andrew Wicklund,
Mark Popich, Henry
Yiu, Lauren
DiRusso, Ed Lee
Client
Seattle
SuperSonics
Software/Hardware
QuarkXPress,
Adobe Photoshop

0567
Art Director
Jack Anderson
Designers
Jack Anderson,
Elmer dela Cruz,
Henry Yiu, Belinda
Bowling, Jay
Hilburn, Beckon
Wyld, Jeff Wolff
Client
Washington
Wizards
Software/Hardware
QuarkXPress,
Adobe Photoshop

0568
Art Director
Jack Anderson
Designers
Jack Anderson,
Andrew Wicklund,
Mark Popich, Henry
Yiu, Lauren
DiRusso, Ed Lee
Client
Seattle
SuperSonics
Software/Hardware
QuarkXPress,
Adobe Photoshop

0569
Art Director
Jack Anderson
Designers
Jack Anderson,
Elmer dela Cruz,
Henry Yiu, Belinda
Bowling, Jay
Hilburn, Beckon
Wyld, Jeff Wolff
Client
Washington
Wizards
Software/Hardware
QuarkXPress,
Adobe Photoshop

0914
Art Director
Jack Anderson
Designers
Jack Anderson,
Sonja Max, James
Tee, Tiffany Place,
Elmer dela Cruz,
Jana Nishi
Client
TerraVida Coffee
Software/Hardware
Adobe Photoshop

0922
Art Directors
Jack Anderson,
Larry Anderson
Designers
Larry Anderson,
Elmer dela Cruz,
Bruce Stigler, Jay
Hilburn, Dorothee
Soechting, Don
Stayner
Client
Widmer Brothers

0925
Art Director
Jack Anderson
Designers
Jack Anderson,
Andrew Wicklund,
Henry Yiu, Andrew
Smith, Bruce
Branson-Meyer,
John Anderle
Client
PMI

Hoyne Design

0399
Art Director
Andrew Hoyne
Designer
Andrew Hoyne
Client
Schiavello
Software/Hardware
Adobe Illustrator
Font
Hand drawn

0897
Art Director
Andrew Hoyne
Designer
James West
Client
BMG Music
Australia
Software/Hardware
QuarkXPress,
Adobe Photoshop,
Adobe Illustrator
Fonts
Mrs Eaves,
Helvetica Neue,
hand drawn

0965
Art Director
Andrew Hoyne
Designer
James West
Client
Nike Australia
Software/Hardware
Adobe Illustrator
Font
Hand drawn

0968
Art Director
Andrew Hoyne
Designer
James West
Client
Nike Australia
Software/Hardware
Adobe Illustrator
Font
Hand drawn

0982
Art Director
Andrew Hoyne
Designers
Andrew Hoyne,
David Marinelli
Client
Il Fornalo
Software/Hardware
Adobe Illustrator,
Adobe Photoshop
Font
Hand drawn

IAAH/ iamalways hungry

0139
Art Director
Nessim Higson
Designers
Nessim Higson,
Chuck Wooding
Client
Self promotion,
Chuck Wooding
Software/Hardware
QuarkXPress,
Adobe Illustrator,
Adobe Photoshop
Font
Mrs Eaves,
Helvetica Neue
(condensed)

0167
Art Director
Nessim Higson
Designer
Nessim Higson
Client
Self promotion,
personal
Software/Hardware
QuarkXPress,
Adobe Illustrator
Font
Didot

0730
Art Director
Nessim Higson
Designer
Nessim Higson
Client
Self promotion,
IAAH
Software/Hardware
Adobe Photoshop
Fonts
Mrs Eaves, Didot

0778
Art Director
Nessim Higson
Designer
Nessim Higson
Client
AIGA Birmingham
Software/Hardware
Adobe Illustrator
Fonts
Futura, Knockout,
Rosewood,
Decolade

0936
Art Director
Nessim Higson
Designer
Nessim Higson
Client
Genex
Software/Hardware
Adobe Photoshop,
Adobe Illustrator
Fonts
HTF Knockout,
Helvetica,
Clarendon

Ideation Signs & Communi- cations, Inc.

0009
Art Director
Kacha Azema
Designer
Kacha Azema
Client
Rustproof Youth
Ministries
Software/Hardware
Adobe Illustrator
Fonts
Hand drawn,
customized

0010
Art Director
Kacha Azema
Designer
Kacha Azema
Client
Rustproof Youth
Ministries
Software/Hardware
Adobe Illustrator
Fonts
Hand drawn,
customized

0011
Art Director
Kacha Azema
Designer
Kacha Azema
Client
Rustproof Youth
Ministries
Software/Hardware
Adobe Illustrator
Fonts
Hand drawn,
customized

Insight Design Communic ations

0145
Art Director
Tracy Holdeman
Designer
Lea Carmichael
Client
YAAA
Software/Hardware
Freehand
Fonts
Badhouse,
Alternate Gothic

0815
Art Director
Tracy Holdeman
Designer
Lea Carmichael
Client
Public Relations
Society of America
Software/Hardware
Freehand, Adobe
Photoshop
Fonts
Redfive, Robotik,
Epokha, P22 Sinel

Yanek Iontef

0033
Art Director
Yanek Iontef
Designer
Yanek Iontef
Client
Yanek Iontef
Software/Hardware
Macromedia
Fontographer,
Freehand
Font
Erica (Hebrew)

0034
Art Director
Yanek Iontef
Designer
Yanek Iontef
Client
Pauza Products and
Services Ltd.
Software/Hardware
Macromedia
Fontographer,
Freehand
Font
Pauza
(Hebrew, Latin)

0238
Art Director
Yanek Iontef
Designer
Yanek Iontef
Client
FSI—Font Shop
International
Software/Hardware
Freehand
Font
FF Cartonnage—
Alternate, Roman,
Pict

0239
Art Director
Yanek Iontef
Designer
Yanek Iontef
Client
FSI—Font Shop
International
Software/Hardware
Freehand
Font
FF Cartonnage—
Alternate, Roman,
Pict

0240
Art Director
Yanek Iontef
Designer
Yanek Iontef
Client
FSI—Font Shop
International
Software/Hardware
Freehand

Font
FF Cartonnage—
Alternate, Roman,
Pict

0241
Art Director
Yanek Iontef
Designer
Yanek Iontef
Client
FSI—Font Shop
International
Software/Hardware
Freehand
Font
FF Cartonnage—
Alternate, Roman,
Pict

0242
Art Director
Yanek Iontef
Designer
Yanek Iontef
Client
FSI—Font Shop
International
Software/Hardware
Freehand
Font
FF Cartonnage—
Alternate, Roman,
Pict

0243
Art Director
Yanek Iontef
Designer
Yanek Iontef
Client
FSI—Font Shop
International
Software/Hardware
Freehand
Font
FF Cartonnage—
Alternate, Roman,
Pict

0244
Art Director
Yanek Iontef
Designer
Yanek Iontef
Client
FSI—Font Shop
International
Software/Hardware
Freehand
Font
FF Cartonnage—
Alternate, Roman,
Pict

0408
Art Director
Yanek Iontef
Designer
Yanek Iontef
Client
Yanek Iontef
Software/Hardware
Freehand
Font
FF Cartonnage—
Alternate, Roman,
Pict

0786
Art Director
Yanek Iontef
Designer
Yanek Iontef
Client
GESHER Theatre
(Russian and
Hebrew speaking
theatre)

Font
FF Cartonnage—
Alternate, Roman,
Pict

Software/Hardware
Freehand, Adobe
Photoshop
Fonts
Helvetica (Cyrillic),
Nakris Tam (Hebrew)

0872
Art Director
Yanek Iontef
Designer
Yanek Iontef
Client
Yanek Iontef
Software/Hardware
Freehand, Adobe
Photoshop
Fonts
Sixty Seven
(Hebrew),
Colony (Hebrew)

0873
Art Director
Yanek Iontef
Designer
Yanek Iontef
Client
Tel Aviv Museum
of Art
Software/Hardware
Freehand, Adobe
Photoshop
Font
Bell Gothic (Latin),
Haim (Hebrew)

IRBE Design

0772
Art Director
Igors Irbe
Client
IRBE Design
Software/Hardware
QuarkXPress,
Adobe Photoshop
Paper/Materials
Gilbert Clear Vellum

iridium, a design agency

0717
Art Directors
Jean-Luc Denat,
Mario L'Ecuyer
Designer
Mario L'Ecuyer
Client
Mitel Corporation
Software/Hardware
QuarkXPress,
Adobe Photoshop
Paper/Materials
Graphika Lineal,
Potlatch McCoy
Gloss, French Paper
Construction

0743
Designer
Etienne Bessette
Client
Epsilon
Software/Hardware
QuarkXPress,
Adobe Illustrator,
Adobe Photoshop
Paper/Materials
Sappi Horizon Silk

Iron Design

0138
Art Director
Todd Edmunds
Designer
Xanthe Matychak
Client
Iron Design
Software/Hardware
Adobe Illustrator
Fonts
Helvetica,
Signpainter

0842
Art Director
Todd Edmunds
Designer
Louis Johnson
Client
AIDS Work (Souther
Tier Aids Program)
Software/Hardware
Adobe Photoshop,
Adobe Illustrator
Fonts
Clarendon, Parapa
Display Caps,
Poplar Black,
Vingta, Runic,
Slot SSK

Jan Family

0067
Designer
Soffi Beier
Font
Based on
Helvetica Neue

0072
Designer
Soffi Beier
Font
Based on
Helvetica Neue

0220
Designer
Soffi Beier
Font
Based on
Helvetica Neue

0253
Designer
Soffi Beier
Font
Based on
Helvetica Neue

0254
Designer
Soffi Beier
Font
Based on
Helvetica Neue

0257
Designer
Soffi Beier
Font
Based on
Helvetica Neue

Jason Gomez

0097
Art Director
Jason Gomez
Designer
Jason Gomez
Client
Joanna Schulz

Software/Hardware
Adobe Illustrator,
Adobe Photoshop
Fonts
Bickham Script,
Bembo Expert,
customized

Joe Miller's Company

0004
Designer
Joe Miller
Client
Works/San Jose
Software/Hardware
Adobe Photoshop,
QuarkXPress
Font
Akzidenz Grotesk

0096
Designer
Joe Miller
Client
Works/San Jose
Software/Hardware
Adobe Photoshop,
QuarkXPress
Fonts
Didot, Bauer Bodoni

0368
Designer
Joe Miller
Client
Works/San Jose
Software/Hardware
Adobe Illustrator,
Adobe Photoshop,
QuarkXPress

0442
Designer
Joe Miller
Client
Poetry Center San
Jose
Software/Hardware
Adobe Illustrator
Fonts
Mrs Eaves,
Helvetica, Times,
customized

0529
Designer
Joe Miller
Client
Association for
Viet Arts
Software/Hardware
Adobe Photoshop,
QuarkXPress
Font
Akzidenz Grotesk

0773
Designer
Joe Miller
Client
Works/San Jose
Software/Hardware
Adobe Photoshop,
Adobe Illustrator
Font
Helvetica

0838
Designer
Joe Miller
Client
Works/San Jose
Software/Hardware
Adobe Photoshop,
QuarkXPress
Fonts
Baskerville,
Akzidenz Grotesk

0839
Designer
Joe Miller
Client
Works/San Jose
Software/Hardware
Adobe Illustrator,
QuarkXPress
Fonts
Stroke, Century

0855
Designer
Joe Miller
Client
Works/San Jose
Software/Hardware
Adobe Illustrator,
Adobe Photoshop,
Streamline,
QuarkXPress
Fonts
Presstype,
hand drawn

0880
Designer
Joe Miller
Client
Works/San Jose
Software/Hardware
Adobe Photoshop,
Adobe Illustrator,
QuarkXPress
Font
Akzidenz Grotesk

Johann A. Gomez

0401
Art Director
Johann A. Gomez
Designer
Johann A. Gomez
Client
Replicant Wear
Software/Hardware
Adobe Illustrator,
Adobe Photoshop
Font
Customized

0431
Art Director
Johann A. Gomez
Designer
Johann A. Gomez
Client
Microsoft
Software/Hardware
Adobe Illustrator,
Adobe Photoshop
Font
Customized

0461
Art Director
Johann A. Gomez
Designer
Johann A. Gomez
Client
Black Panties
Software/Hardware
Adobe Illustrator,
Freehand, Adobe
Photoshop
Font
Customized

Johnson Banks

0194
Art Director
Michael Johnson
Designers
Julia Woollams,
Kater Hudball

Client
Conran Octopus
Software/Hardware
QuarkXPress
Paper/Materials
Cloth, machine

0223
Art Director
Michael Johnson
Designers
Julia Woollams,
Kater Hudball
Client
Conran Octopus
Software/Hardware
QuarkXPress
Paper/Materials
Cloth, machine

Jones Design Group

0104
Art Director
Vicky Jones
Designers
Katherine Staggs,
Brody Boye
Client
Jones Design
Group
Software/Hardware
QuarkXPress,
Adobe Illustrator
Paper/Materials
Tattoos

Juan Torneros

0792
Art Director
Juan Torneros
Designer
Juan Torneros
Client
Universidad
Nacional de
Colombia
Software/Hardware
Freehand, Adobe
Photoshop
Font
TV Screen Fonts,
Zurich

0826
Art Director
Juan Torneros
Designer
Juan Torneros
Client
Universidad
Nacional de
Colombia
Software/Hardware
Freehand, Adobe
Photoshop
Font
TV Screen Fonts,
Zurich

0882
Art Director
Juan Torneros
Designer
Juan Torneros
Client
Universidad
Nacional de
Colombia
Software/Hardware
Freehand, Adobe
Photoshop

Font
TV Screen Fonts,
Zurich

Juicy Temples Creative

0370
Art Director
Klaus Heesch
Designers
Randy J. Hunt,
Ross Pike
Client
Juicy Temples
Creative
Software/Hardware
Adobe Illustrator
Font
CA Aires

0425
Art Director
Klaus Heesch
Designers
Randy J. Hunt,
Ross Pike
Client
Juicy Temples
Creative
Software/Hardware
Adobe Illustrator

0957
Art Director
Klaus Heesch
Designers
Anthony DeLaura,
Randy J. Hunt
Client
Juicy Temples
Creative
Software/Hardware
Flash, Adobe
Illustrator
Fonts
CA Aires, Urban,
Mini

0958
Art Director
Klaus Heesch
Designers
Anthony DeLaura,
Randy J. Hunt
Client
Juicy Temples
Creative
Software/Hardware
Flash, Adobe
Illustrator

0959
Art Director
Klaus Heesch
Designers
Anthony DeLaura,
Randy J. Hunt
Client
Juicy Temples
Creative
Software/Hardware
Flash, Adobe
Illustrator

0960
Art Director
Klaus Heesch
Designers
Anthony DeLaura,
Randy J. Hunt
Client
Juicy Temples
Creative
Software/Hardware
Flash, Adobe
Illustrator

Karim Rashid Inc.

0433
Art Director
Valeria Bianco
Designers
Karim Rashid,
Valeria Bianco
Software/Hardware
Soildworks, Formz,
Adobe Photoshop,
Adobe Illustrator

0434
Art Director
Valeria Bianco
Designers
Karim Rashid,
Valeria Bianco
Software/Hardware
Soildworks, Formz,
Adobe Photoshop,
Adobe Illustrator

0437
Art Director
Valeria Bianco
Designers
Karim Rashid,
Valeria Bianco
Software/Hardware
Soildworks, Formz,
Adobe Photoshop,
Adobe Illustrator

0441
Art Director
Valeria Bianco
Designers
Karim Rashid,
Valeria Bianco
Software/Hardware
Soildworks, Formz,
Adobe Photoshop,
Adobe Illustrator

Kearney Rocholl Corporate Communications AG

0390
Art Director
Frank Rocholl
Designer
Frank Rocholl
Client
Vividrprojects
GmbH
Software/Hardware
Freehand
Font
Platelet

0391
Art Director
Frank Rocholl
Designer
Frank Rocholl
Client
Hype Mag.
Software/Hardware
Freehand
Font
FF Jigger

0392
Art Director
Frank Rocholl
Designer

Frank Rocholl
Client
DBV Winterthur
Versicherung
Software/Hardware
Freehand
Font
Digital

0393
Art Director
Frank Rocholl
Designer
Frank Rocholl
Client
I-TV-T AG
Software/Hardware
Freehand
Fonts
Bell Gothic, OCRA

0394
Art Director
Frank Rocholl
Designer
Frank Rocholl
Client
Audi AG
Software/Hardware
Freehand
Font
Univers (Extended)

0395
Art Director
Frank Rocholl
Designer
Frank Rocholl
Client
Area Project
Development Ltd,
London
Software/Hardware
Freehand
Font
Sackers Gothic,
Officina

0718
Art Director
Frank Rocholl
Designer
Frank Rocholl
Client
Prof. Tom
Philipps/Rocholl
Projects Folder
Software/Hardware
Freehand
Font
Univers
(Condensed)

0719
Art Director
Frank Rocholl
Designer
Dmitri Lavrow
Client
Moller Design
Software/Hardware
QuarkXPress
Font
Typestar

0720
Art Director
Frank Rocholl
Designer
Dmitri Lavrow
Client
Moller Design
Software/Hardware
QuarkXPress
Font
Typestar

0724
Art Director

Frank Rocholl
Designer
Frank Rocholl
Client
Area Project
Development Ltd,
London
Software/Hardware
Freehand, Adobe
Photoshop
Font
FF Jigger

0726
Art Director
Frank Rocholl
Designer
Michel Schmidt
Client
Hype Mag.
Software/Hardware
Freehand, Adobe
Photoshop
Font
FF Jigger,
Pastelaria

0737
Art Director
Frank Rocholl
Designer
Frank Rocholl
Client
KearneyRocholl
Software/Hardware
Freehand
Font
Nuri (by Frank
Rocholl)

0825
Art Director
Frank Rocholl
Designer
Frank Rocholl
Client
FH Darmstadt
University of
Applied Science
Software/Hardware
Freehand, Adobe
Photoshop
Fonts
Signature
Development
(headline),
FF Hardcase (copy)

0837
Art Director
Frank Rocholl
Designer
Frank Rocholl
Client
Levi Straus
Germany
Software/Hardware
Freehand
Fonts
Avant Garde,
Franklin Gothic,
Decorated,
Astonished,
Boomshaker

0840
Art Director
Frank Rocholl
Designer
Frank Rocholl
Client
Levi Straus
Germany
Software/Hardware
Freehand
Fonts
Avant Garde,
Franklin Gothic,
Decorated,
Astonished,
Boomshaker

0859
Art Director
Frank Rocholl
Designer
Frank Rocholl
Client
Levi Straus
Germany
Software/Hardware
Freehand
Fonts
Avant Garde,
Franklin Gothic,
Decorated,
Astonished,
Boomshaker

0861
Art Director
Frank Rocholl
Designer
Frank Rocholl
Client
KearneyRocholl
Software/Hardware
Freehand
Fonts
Avant Garde,
Franklin Gothic,
Decorated,
Astonished,
Boomshaker

0862
Art Director
Frank Rocholl
Designer
Frank Rocholl
Client
Levi Straus
Germany
Software/Hardware
Freehand
Fonts
Avant Garde,
Franklin Gothic,
Decorated,
Astonished,
Boomshaker

0863
Art Director
Frank Rocholl
Designer
Frank Rocholl
Client
Levi Straus
Germany
Software/Hardware
Freehand
Fonts
Avant Garde,
Franklin Gothic,
Decorated,
Astonished,
Boomshaker

0885
Art Director
Frank Rocholl
Designer
Michel Schmidt
Client
Dittmar GmbH &
Co. KG
Software/Hardware
Freehand, Adobe
Photoshop
Fonts
Dirty Ego, Diesel,
Orator

0887
Art Director
Frank Rocholl
Designer

Michel Schmidt
Client
Dittmar GmbH &
Co. KG
Software/Hardware
Freehand, Adobe
Photoshop
Fonts
Dirty Ego, Diesel,
Orator

0985
Art Director
Frank Rocholl
Designer
Heiko Gimbel
Client
Rocholl Pojects
Software/Hardware
Freehand, Adobe
Photoshop, Flash,
Dreamweaver
Fonts
News Gothic,
Schild 7

0988
Art Director
Frank Rocholl
Designer
Heiko Gimbel
Client
Rocholl Pojects
Software/Hardware
Freehand, Adobe
Photoshop, Flash,
Dreamweaver
Fonts
News Gothic,
Schild 7

Kessels Kramer

0697
Art Director
Erik Kessels

Kinetic Singapore

0444
Art Directors
Pann Lim, Leng
Soh, Roy Poh
Designers
Pann Lim, Leng
Soh, Roy Poh
Client
Kinetic Singapore
Software/Hardware
Freehand
Paper/Materials
Woodfree Paper

Kolegram Design

0075
Art Director
Mike Teixeira
Designer
Mike Teixeira
Client
Kolegram Design
Software/Hardware
QuarkXPress

Kontour Design

0103
Art Director
Sibylle Hagmann

Designer
Sibylle Hagmann
Client
Museum of Fine
Arts Houston, USA
Software/Hardware
Adobe InDesign
Fonts
Council, Tarzana

0228
Art Director
Sibylle Hagmann
Designer
Sibylle Hagmann
Client
Dallas Museum
of Art, USA
Software/Hardware
QuarkXPress
Fonts
Dalliance,
Foundry Gridnik

0278
Art Director
Sibylle Hagmann
Designer
Sibylle Hagmann
Client
Dallas Museum of
Art, USA
Software/Hardware
QuarkXPress

0633
Art Director
Sibylle Hagmann
Designer
Sibylle Hagmann
Client
Museum of Fine
Arts Houston, USA
Software/Hardware
Adobe InDesign
Fonts
Council, Brea

0634
Art Director
Sibylle Hagmann
Designer
Sibylle Hagmann
Client
Émigré,
Sacramento, CA,
Software/Hardware
QuarkXPress
Font
Cholla

Kontrapunkt

0146
Art Director
Peter Van Toorn
Brix
Designers
Bo Linnemann,
Peter Van Toorn Brix
Client
Billung Airport
Software/Hardware
Adobe Illustrator,
Fontographer
Font
Customized

0402
Art Director
Eduard Cehovin
Designer
Eduard Cehovin
Client
Ivana Wineham
Software/Hardware
A1

0403
Art Director
Peter Van Toorn
Brix
Designers
Morten Sornsen,
Peter Van Toorn Brix
Client
Semler

0404
Art Director
Bo Linnemann
Designer
Bo Linnemann
Client
Dansre Bank

KOREK Studio

0380
Art Director
Wojtek Koruc
KOREK
Designer
Wojtek Korkuc
KOREK
Client
Transforma Ltd.
Software/Hardware
Collage, Adobe
Photoshop
Fonts
Helvetica, Acculs

KROG

0680
Art Director
Edi Berk
Designer
Edi Berk
Client
Obrtna zbornica
Slovenije, Ljubljana
Software/Hardware
QuarkXPress,
Adobe Illustrator,
Adobe Photoshop
Fonts
Garamond ITC,
Franklin

Frida Larios

0821
Art Director
Frida Larios
Designer
Frida Larios
Client
Self-initiated project
Software/Hardware
Adobe Illustrator

Ligalux GmbH

0124
Art Directors
Petra Matouschek,
Martina Massong
Designers
Martina Massong,
Vicky Abndt
Client
Fischer Appelt
Kommunikation,
GmbH
Software/Hardware
QuarkXPress,
Freehand
Fonts
DTL Elzevire,
Helvetica Neue

0169
Art Directors
Petra Matouschek,
Martina Massong
Designers
Martina Massong,
Vicky Abndt
Client
Fischer Appelt
Kommunikation,
GmbH
Software/Hardware
QuarkXPress,
Freehand
Fonts
DTL Elzevire,
Helvetica Neue

0207
Art Director
Claudia
Fischer-Appel
Designers
Claudia Fischer-
Appel, Lars Nieb
Client
Ligalux GmbH
Software/Hardware
Freehand
Paper/Materials
Munken &
Luxomagi

0318
Art Director
Claudia
Fischer-Appel
Designers
Claudia Fischer-
Appel, Lars Nieb
Client
Ligalux GmbH
Software/Hardware
Freehand
Paper/Materials
Munken &
Luxomagi

0324
Art Director
Claudia
Fischer-Appel
Designers
Claudia Fischer-
Appel, Lars Nieb
Client
Ligalux GmbH
Software/Hardware
Freehand
Paper/Materials
Munken &
Luxomagi

0325
Art Director
Claudia
Fischer-Appel
Designers
Claudia Fischer-
Appel, Lars Nieb
Client
Ligalux GmbH
Software/Hardware
Freehand
Paper/Materials
Munken &
Luxomagi

0326
Art Director
Claudia
Fischer-Appel
Designers
Claudia Fischer-
Appel, Lars Nieb
Client
Ligalux GmbH

Software/Hardware
Freehand
Paper/Materials
Munken &
Luxomagi

0327
Art Director
Claudia
Fischer-Appel
Designers
Claudia Fischer-
Appel, Lars Nieb
Client
Ligalux GmbH
Software/Hardware
Freehand
Paper/Materials
Munken &
Luxomagi

0334
Art Director
Claudia
Fischer-Appel
Designers
Claudia Fischer-
Appel, Lars Nieb
Client
Ligalux GmbH
Software/Hardware
Freehand
Paper/Materials
Munken &
Luxomagi

0335
Art Director
Claudia
Fischer-Appel
Designers
Claudia Fischer-
Appel, Lars Nieb
Client
Ligalux GmbH
Software/Hardware
Freehand
Paper/Materials
Munken &
Luxomagi

0336
Art Director
Claudia
Fischer-Appel
Designers
Claudia Fischer-
Appel, Lars Nieb
Client
Ligalux GmbH
Software/Hardware
Freehand
Paper/Materials
Munken &
Luxomagi

0337
Art Director
Claudia
Fischer-Appel
Designers
Claudia Fischer-
Appel, Lars Nieb
Client
Ligalux GmbH
Software/Hardware
Freehand
Paper/Materials
Munken &
Luxomagi

0338
Art Director
Claudia
Fischer-Appel
Designers
Claudia Fischer-
Appel, Lars Nieb
Client
Ligalux GmbH

Software/Hardware
Freehand
Software/Hardware
Freehand
Paper/Materials
Munken &
Luxomagi

0339
Art Director
Claudia
Fischer-Appel
Designers
Claudia Fischer-
Appel, Lars Nieb
Client
Ligalux GmbH
Software/Hardware
Freehand
Paper/Materials
Munken &
Luxomagi

0340/0366
Art Director
Claudia
Fischer-Appel
Designers
Claudia Fischer-
Appel, Lars Nieb
Client
Ligalux GmbH
Software/Hardware
Freehand
Paper/Materials
Munken &
Luxomagi

0681
Art Director
Petra Matouschek
Designer
Behruz
Tschaitschian
Client
Augusta
Technologie AG
Software/Hardware
QuarkXPress,
Freehand
Fonts
Bembo, Chalet
Colgne

0682
Art Director
Martina Massong
Designer
Martina Massong
Client
Dentist's Practice
Sattler and Jakel
Software/Hardware
QuarkXPress
Fonts
Alternate Gothic,
Bembo

0683
Art Director
Petra Matouschek
Designers
Christian Dworak,
Meike Teubner
Client
Bundesknappschaft
Software/Hardware
QuarkXPress,
Freehand
Fonts
DTL Prokyon,
Profile, Zurich

0684
Art Director
Petra Matouschek
Designers
Christian Dworak,
Meike Teubner

Client
Bundesknappschaf
Software/Hardware
QuarkXPress,
Freehand

0698
Art Director
Petra Matouschek
Designer
Behruz
Tschaitschian
Client
Augusta
Technologie AG
Software/Hardware
QuarkXPress,
Freehand

0699
Art Director
Petra Matouschek
Designer
Behruz
Tschaitschian
Client
Augusta
Technologie AG
Software/Hardware
QuarkXPress,
Freehand

0700
Art Director
Petra Matouschek
Designer
Behruz
Tschaitschian
Client
Augusta
Technologie AG
Software/Hardware
QuarkXPress,
Freehand

0701
Art Director
Petra Matouschek
Designer
Behruz
Tschaitschian
Client
Augusta
Technologie AG
Software/Hardware
QuarkXPress,
Freehand

0702
Art Directors
Petra Matouschek,
Martina Massong
Designers
Martina Massong,
Vicky Abndt
Client
Fischer Appelt
Kommunikation,
GmbH
Software/Hardware
QuarkXPress,
Freehand
Fonts
DTL Elzevire,
Helvetica Neue

0703
Art Director
Hedda Gerdes
Designer
Sylvia Kossmann
Client
MSD Sharp &
Dohme